the
Apostles'
Creed

the Apostles' Creed

A. W. TOZER

Compiled by Kevin Mungons

MOODY PUBLISHERS
CHICAGO

Compiled and edited by Kevin Mungons
Interior design: Brandi Davis
Cover design: Erik M. Peterson

ISBN: 978-0-8024-2973-5

Originally delivered by fleets of horse-drawn wagons, the affordable paperbacks from D. L. Moody's publishing house resourced the church and served everyday people. Now, after more than 125 years of publishing and ministry, Moody Publishers' mission remains the same—even if our delivery systems have changed a bit. For more information on other books (and resources) created from a biblical perspective, go to www.moodypublishers.com or write to:

Moody Publishers
820 N. LaSalle Boulevard
Chicago, IL 60610

1 3 5 7 9 10 8 6 4 2

Printed in the United States of America

CONTENTS

Part Two: Living Out the Creed

EATOR OF HEAVEN AND EARTH; AND IN JESUS CHR

S   ONLY   SON,   OUR   LO

HO   WAS   CONCEIVED   BY   THE   HOLY   SPIR

RN   FROM   THE   VIRGIN   MA

FFERED   UNDER   PONTIUS   PILA

AS   CRUCIFIED,   DEAD   AND   BURI

SCENDED   INTO   HELL,   ON   THE   THIRD

SE   AGAIN   FROM   THE   DE

CENDED   TO   HEAV

TS   AT   THE   RIGHT   H

F   GOD   THE   FATHER   ALMIGH

ENCE   HE   WILL   COME   TO   JU

E   LIVING   AND   THE   DE

BELIEVE   IN   THE   HOLY   SPI

E   HOLY   CATHOLIC   CHUR

E   COMMUNION   OF   SAIN

E   REMISSION   OF   SI

E   RESURRECTION   OF   THE   FLE

The early Christians, under the fire of persecution,

driven from place to place,

sometimes deprived of the opportunity

for careful instruction in the faith,

wanted a "rule" that would sum up

all that they must believe to assure their everlasting welfare.

Out of this critical need arose the creeds.

Of the many, the Apostles' Creed

is the best known and best loved,

and has been reverently repeated

by the largest number of believers

through the centuries.

— A. W. Tozer

THE APOSTLES' CREED

I BELIEVE in God the Father Almighty,

maker of heaven and earth:

And in Jesus Christ his only Son our Lord:

Who was conceived by the Holy Ghost,

Born of the Virgin Mary: Suffered under Pontius Pilate,

was crucified, dead, and buried:

He descended into hell;

The third day he rose again from the dead:

He ascended into heaven,

And sitteth on the right hand of God the Father Almighty:

From thence he shall come to judge the quick and the dead.

I believe in the Holy Ghost:

The holy catholic church; The communion of saints:

The forgiveness of sins: The resurrection of the body:

And the life everlasting. Amen.

EATOR OF HEAVEN AND EARTH; AND IN JESUS CHR

S   ONLY   SON,   OUR   LO

HO   WAS   CONCEIVED   BY   THE   HOLY   SPIR

RN   FROM   THE   VIRGIN   MA

FFERED   UNDER   PONTIUS   PILA

S   CRUCIFIED,   DEAD   AND   BURI

SCENDED   INTO   HELL,   ON   THE   THIRD

SE   AGAIN   FROM   THE   DE

CENDED   TO   HEAV

TS   AT   THE   RIGHT   HA

GOD   THE   FATHER   ALMIGH

ENCE   HE   WILL   COME   TO   JUD

E   LIVING   AND   THE   DEA

BELIEVE   IN   THE   HOLY   SPIR

E   HOLY   CATHOLIC   CHURC

E   COMMUNION   OF   SAIN

E   REMISSION   OF   SIN

E   RESURRECTION   OF   THE   FLES

TOZER'S CREED

A. W. TOZER loved the classic Christian creeds and wrote about them frequently. He called the Apostles' Creed "the best known and best loved . . . reverently repeated by the largest number of believers through the centuries. And for millions of good people, that creed contains the essentials of truth."

But Tozer preached and taught in an era when creedal statements were increasingly suspect. Various Christian movements were founded with "no creed but the Bible," an idea that became the rallying cry for a certain segment of the evangelical church. John Oxenham summed up these sentiments in "Credo," a popular poem that declared "Not what, but WHOM! For Christ is more than all the creeds."

Tozer quickly pointed out that this aversion to creedal statements was, in fact, a belief system of its own, what he called the "no-creed creed." Tozer saw this trend as a danger, containing a few grains of real truth buried beneath "a mighty pile of chaff." A full century earlier, Samuel Miller had predicted that "whenever a group of men began to slide, with respect to orthodoxy, they generally attempted to break, if not to conceal, their fall, by declaiming against creeds and confessions."

As an antidote, Tozer preached the primary importance of basic doctrine in the believer's life. "Hold fast to the word I preached to you . . . ," Paul said. "For I delivered to you as of first importance what I also received: that Christ died for our sins in accordance with the Scriptures" (1 Cor. 15:2–3 ESV). This doctrinal integrity was entrusted to the church and to pastors, as seen in Paul's advice to young Timothy: "Take heed unto thyself, and unto the doctrine" (1 Tim. 4:16). And for Tozer, "the truth shared by saints in the apostolic fellowship is the same truth that is outlined for convenience in the Apostles' Creed."

This collection of essays gathers Tozer's best writing about the creeds and creedal ideas, curated from his sermons, magazine articles, and books. Tozer believed the creeds would pull evangelicals toward a doctrinal consensus, a better understanding of what was truly essential to the orthodox faith. Or negatively stated, the creeds avoided *unessential* details. Though he appreciated fully developed theological systems, he expressed exasperation about contemporary controversies such as the precise timing of end-time events. Ultimately, Tozer defended every article of the traditional creed text, even the phrase "He descended into hell," though many evangelicals would later drop this line.

Those who are encountering A. W. Tozer for the first time will note his tendency to quote Christians from past eras—and not just familiar names like Luther, Wesley, and Finney. Tozer read deeply, and expected readers to follow his passing references to Bernard of Cluny, Richard Rolle, and Gerhard Tersteegen. He did so without apology, noting that early Methodist hymns, full of intense theology and obscure language, were intended for "farmers and sheep herders and cattle ranchers, coal miners and blacksmiths, carpenters and cotton pickers."

Those who are more familiar with Tozer's literary legacy might recognize a certain irony. Though he spoke of the creeds with some frequency, they were not part of his denomination's worship tradition. His Chicago church recited the Apostles' Creed for a time, then stopped, and he hesitated to recommend the practice for anyone.

"This is not to plead for the use of the historic creeds in our Christian gatherings," Tozer says in the prologue to this collection. "I realize that it is entirely possible to recite the Apostles' Creed every Sunday for a lifetime with no profit to the soul . . . they may be learned by rote and repeated without conviction and so be altogether stale and unprofitable."

Such words sound like a disclaimer, or outright warning. The creeds must not point to mere intellectual knowledge—they must be lived out. In the final three essays of this collection, Tozer moves from orthodoxy (right doctrine) to orthopraxy (right living) and orthopathy (right passions). Or as Tozer would put it, "The doctrines of God are to get on their working clothes, get their hammer and their sword, and go out and get busy. That's the purpose of God for His church."

—Kevin Mungons, editor

REATOR OF HEAVEN AND EARTH; AND IN JESUS CHR

S   ONLY   SON,   OUR   LO

HO   WAS   CONCEIVED   BY   THE   HOLY   SPIR

ORN   FROM   THE   VIRGIN   MA

FFERED   UNDER   PONTIUS   PILA

AS   CRUCIFIED,   DEAD   AND   BURI

SCENDED   INTO   HELL,   ON   THE   THIRD

SE   AGAIN   FROM   THE   DE

CENDED   TO   HEAV

TS   AT   THE   RIGHT   HA

GOD   THE   FATHER   ALMIGH

ENCE   HE   WILL   COME   TO   JU

E   LIVING   AND   THE   DE

BELIEVE   IN   THE   HOLY   SPIR

E   HOLY   CATHOLIC   CHUR

E   COMMUNION   OF   SAIN

E   REMISSION   OF   SI

E   RESURRECTION   OF   THE   FLES

WHY THE CREEDS ARE STILL IMPORTANT TODAY

Among certain Christians it has become quite the fashion to cry down creed and cry up experience as the only true test of Christianity. The expression "Not creed, but Christ" (taken, I believe, from a poem by John Oxenham) has been widely accepted as the very voice of truth and given a place alongside the writings of prophets and apostles.

When I first heard the words, they sounded good. One got from them the idea that the advocates of the no-creed creed had found a precious secret that the rest of us had missed; that they had managed to cut right through the verbiage of historic Christianity and come direct to Christ without bothering about doctrine. And the words appeared to honor our Lord more perfectly by focusing attention upon Him alone and not upon mere words. But is this true? I think not.

In this no-creed creed there are indeed a few grains of real truth, but not as many as the no-creed advocates imagine. And those few are buried beneath a mighty pile of chaff, something that the no-creed people cannot at all imagine.

Now I have a lot of sympathy for the no-creed creedalists, for I realize that they are protesting the substitution of a dead creed for a living Christ; and in this I join them wholeheartedly. But this antithesis need not exist; there is no reason for our creeds being dead just as there is no reason for our faith being dead. James tells us that there is such a thing as dead faith, but we do not reject all faith for that reason.

Now the truth is that creed is implicit in every thought, word, or act of the Christian life. It is altogether impossible to come to Christ without knowing at least something about Him; and what we know about Him is what we believe about Him; and what we believe about Him is our Christian creed. Otherwise stated, since our creed is what we believe, it is impossible to believe on Christ and have no creed.

> *Creed is implicit in every thought, word, or act of the Christian life. . . . It is impossible to believe on Christ and have no creed.*

Preaching Christ is generally, and correctly, held to be the purest, noblest ministry in which any man can engage; but preaching Christ includes a great deal more than talking about Christ in superlatives. It means more than giving vent to the religious love the speaker feels for the person of Christ. Glowing love for Christ will give fragrance and warmth to any sermon, but it is still not enough. Love must be intelligent and informed if it is to have any permanent meaning. The effective sermon must have intellectual content, and wherever there is intellect there is creed. It cannot be otherwise.

This is not to plead for the use of the historic creeds in our Christian gatherings. I realize that it is entirely possible to recite the Apostles' Creed every Sunday for a lifetime with no profit to the soul. The Nicene Creed may be said or sung in every service without benefiting anyone. The standard creeds are a summary of what the Christian professes to believe, and they are excellent as far as they go yet they may be learned by rote and repeated without conviction and so be altogether stale and unprofitable.

While we may worship (and thousands of Christians do) without the use of any formal creed, it is impossible to worship acceptably without some knowledge of the One we seek to worship. And that knowledge is our creed, whether it is very formalized or not. It is not enough to say that we may have a mystical or numinous experience of God without any doctrinal knowledge and that is sufficient. No, it is not sufficient. We must worship in truth as well as in spirit; and truth can be stated, and when it is stated it becomes creed.

The effort to be practicing Christians without knowing what Christianity is about must always fail. The true Christian should be, indeed must be, a theologian. He must know at least something of the wealth of truth revealed in the Holy Scriptures. And he must know it with sufficient clarity to state it and defend his statement. And what can be stated and defended is a creed.

Because the heart of the Christian life is admittedly faith in a Person, Jesus Christ the Lord, it has been relatively easy for some to press the truth out of all proportion and teach that faith in the person of Christ is all that matters. Who Jesus is matters not, who His Father was, whether Jesus is God or man or both, whether or not He accepted the superstitions and errors of His time as true, whether He actually rose again after His passion or was only thought to have done so by His devoted followers—these things are not important, say the no-creed advocates. What is vital is that we believe on Him and try to follow His teachings.

What is overlooked here is that the conflict of Christ with the Pharisees was over the question of *who He was.* His claim to be God stirred the Pharisees to fury. He could have cooled the fire of their anger by backing away from His claim to equality with God, but He refused to do it. And He further taught that faith in Him embraced a belief that He is very God, and that apart from this there could be no salvation for anyone. "He said unto them, Ye are from beneath; I am from above: ye are of this world; I am not of this world. I said therefore unto you, that ye shall die in your sins: for if ye believe not that I am he, ye shall die in your sins" (John 8:23–24).

To believe on Christ savingly means to believe the right things about Christ. There is no escaping this.

part one

THE CREED

REATOR OF HEAVEN AND EARTH; AND IN JESUS CHR

S   ONLY   SON,   OUR   LO

HO   WAS   CONCEIVED   BY   THE   HOLY   SPIF

ORN   FROM   THE   VIRGIN   MA

FFERED   UNDER   PONTIUS   PILA

AS   CRUCIFIED,   DEAD   AND   BURI

SCENDED   INTO   HELL,   ON   THE   THIRD

OSE   AGAIN   FROM   THE   DE

CENDED   TO   HEAV

TS   AT   THE   RIGHT   HA

GOD   THE   FATHER   ALMIGH

ENCE   HE   WILL   COME   TO   JUC

E   LIVING   AND   THE   DE

BELIEVE   IN   THE   HOLY   SPIR

E   HOLY   CATHOLIC   CHUR

E   COMMUNION   OF   SAIN

E   REMISSION   OF   SI

E   RESURRECTION   OF   THE   FLE

GOD THE FATHER

I believe in God the Father Almighty, maker of heaven and earth

There could be no more central or important theme than the character of God. If you trace effect back to cause and that cause back to another cause and so on, back through the long dim corridors of the past until you come to the primordial atom out of which all things were made, you will find the One who made them—you'll find God.

Behind all previous matter, all life, all law, all space, and all time, there is God. God gives to human life its only significance; there isn't any other apart from Him. If you take the concept of God out of the human mind, there is no other reason for being among the living. We are, as Tennyson said, like "sheep or goats / That nourish a blind life within the brain." And we might as well die as sheep unless we have God in our thoughts.

God is the source of all law and morality and goodness, the One that you must believe in before you can deny Him, the One who is the Word and the One that enables us to speak. I'm sure you will see immediately that in attempting a series of messages about the attributes of God we run into that which is difficult above all things.

The famous preacher Sam Jones (who was a Billy Sunday before Billy Sunday's time) said that when the average preacher takes a text it reminds him of an insect trying to carry a bale of cotton. And when I take my text and try to talk about God I feel like that insect; only God can help me.

John Milton started to write a book on the fall of man and his restoration through Jesus Christ our Lord. He was to call his book *Paradise Lost.* But before he dared to write it, he prayed a prayer that I want to pray as well. He prayed to the Spirit and said,

> *And chiefly thou O Spirit, that dost prefer*
> *Before all temples th' upright heart and pure,*
> *Instruct me.*

I'd like to say, with no attempt at morbid humility, that without a pure heart and a surrendered mind, no man can preach worthily about God and no man can hear worthily. No man can hear these things unless God touches him and illuminates him. And so Milton said,

> *Instruct me, for Thou know'st; ...*
> *What in me is dark*
> *Illumine, what is low raise and support;*
> *That to the highth of this great argument*
> *I may assert eternal providence,*
> *And justifie the wayes of God to men.*

Who can speak about the attributes of God—His self-existence, His omniscience, His omnipotence, His transcendence, and so on—who can do that and do it worthily? Who is capable of anything like that? I'm not. So I only have this one hope: As the poor little donkey rebuked the madness of the prophet and as the rooster crowed one night to arouse the apostle and bring him to repentance, so God may take me and use me. As Jesus rode into Jerusalem on the back of the little donkey, so I pray that He may be willing to ride out before the people on such an unworthy instrument as I.

It is utterly necessary that we know this God, this One that John wrote about, this One that the poet speaks about, this One that theology talks about and this One that we're sent to preach and teach about. It is absolutely, utterly, and critically necessary that we know this One, for you see, man fell when he lost his right concept of God.

As long as man trusted God everything was all right; human beings were healthy and holy (or at least innocent), and pure and good. But then the devil came along and threw a question mark into the mind of the woman: "And he said unto the woman, Yea, hath God said . . . ?" (Gen. 3:1). This was equivalent to sneaking around behind God's back and casting doubt on the goodness of God. And then began the progressive degeneration downward.

When the knowledge of God began to go out of the minds of men, we got into the fix that we're in now:

Because that, when they knew God, they glorified him not as God, neither were thankful; but became vain in their imaginations, and their foolish heart was darkened. Professing themselves to be wise, they became fools, and changed the glory of the uncorruptible God into an image made like to corruptible man, and to birds, and fourfooted beasts, and creeping things. Wherefore God also gave them up to uncleanness through the lusts of their own hearts, to dishonour their own bodies between themselves: who changed the truth of God into a lie, and worshipped and served the creature more than the Creator, who is blessed for ever. Amen. For this cause God gave them up unto vile affections: for even their women did change the natural use into that which is against nature: and likewise also the men, leaving the natural use of the woman, burned in their lust one toward another; men with men working that which is unseemly, and receiving in themselves that recompence of their error which was meet. And even as they did not like to retain God in their knowledge, God gave them over to a reprobate mind, to do those things which are not convenient. (Rom. 1:21–28)

That first chapter of Romans ends with a terrible charge of unrighteousness, fornication, wickedness, covetousness, maliciousness, and all the long, black list of crimes and sins that man has been guilty of.

All that came about because man lost his confidence in God. He didn't know God's character. He didn't know what kind of God God was. He got all mixed up about what God was like. Now the only way back is to have restored confidence in God. And the only way to have restored confidence in God is to have restored knowledge of God.

We see this in the text, "And they that know thy name will put their trust in thee" (Ps. 9:10). The word *name* means character, plus reputation. "And they that know *what kind of God thou art* will put their trust in thee." We wonder why we don't have faith; the answer is, faith is confidence in the character of God, and if we don't know what kind of God God is, we can't have faith.

We read books about George Müller and others and try to have faith. But we forget that faith is confidence in God's character. And because we are not aware of what kind of God God is, or what God is like, we cannot have faith. And so we struggle and wait and hope against hope. But faith doesn't come, because we do not know the character of God. "They that know what Thou art like will put their trust in Thee." It's automatic—it comes naturally when we know what kind of God God is.

I'm going to give you a report on the character of God, to tell you what God is like. And if you're listening with a worthy mind, you'll find faith will spring up. Ignorance and unbelief drag faith down, but a restored knowledge of God will bring faith up. I don't suppose there is ever a time in the history of the world when we needed a restored knowledge of God more than we need it now. Bible-believing Christians have made great gains in the last forty years or so. We have more Bibles now than we've ever had—the Bible is a bestseller. We have more Bible schools than we've ever had, ever in the history of the world. Millions of tons of gospel literature are being poured out all the time. There are more missions now than we know what to do with. And evangelism is riding very, very high at the present time. And more people go to church now, believe it or not, than ever went to church before.

Now all that has something in its favor, there's no doubt about it. But you know, a man can learn at the end of the year how his business stands by balancing off his losses with his gains. And while he may have some gains, if he has too many losses he'll be out of business the next year.

Many of the gospel churches have made some gains over the last years, but we've also suffered one great central loss: our lofty concept of God. Christianity rises like an eagle and flies over the top of all the mountain peaks of all the religions of the world, chiefly because of her lofty concept of God, given to us in divine revelation and by the coming of the Son of God to take human flesh and dwell among us. Christianity, the great church, has for centuries lived on the character of God. She's preached God, she's prayed to God, she's declared God, she's honored God, she's elevated God, she's witnessed to God—the triune God.

But in recent times there has been a loss suffered. We've suffered the loss of that high concept of God, and the concept of God handled by the average gospel church now is so low as to be unworthy of God and a disgrace to the church. It is by neglect, degenerate error, and spiritual blindness that some are saying God is their "pardner" or "the man upstairs." One Christian college put out a booklet called "Christ Is My Quarterback"—He always calls the right play. And a certain businessman was quoted as saying, "God's a good fellow and I like Him."

There isn't a Muslim alive in the world who would stoop to calling God a "good fellow." There isn't a Jew, at least no Jew who believes in his religion, that would ever dare to refer that way to the great Yahweh, the One with the incommunicable name. They talk about God respectfully and reverently. But in the gospel churches, God is a "quarterback" and a "good fellow."

I sometimes feel like walking out on a lot that passes for Christianity. They talk about prayer as "going into a huddle with God," as if God is the coach or the quarterback or something; they all gather around, God gives the signal, and away they go. What preposterous abomination! When the Romans sacrificed a sow on the altar in Jerusalem, they didn't commit anything more frightful than when we drag the holy, holy, holy God down and turn Him into a cheap Santa Claus that we can use to get what we want.

Christianity has lost its dignity. And we'll never get it back unless we know the dignified Holy God, who rides on the wings of the wind and makes the clouds His chariots. We have lost the concept of majesty and the art of worship. I got a letter from my good friend Stacy Woods, who was until recently head of Inter-Varsity. And he said this in the closing lines of his letter: "The church is getting away from worship. I wonder if it is because we are getting away from God." I think he's right and I believe that is the answer.

And then our religion has lost its inwardness. For Christianity, if it's anything, is an inward religion. Jesus said that we are to worship in spirit and in truth. And yet we've lost it because we have lost the concept of deity that makes it possible. Even though we've hung on to our Scofield Bible and still believe in the seven main doctrines of the fundamental faith, we've lost the awe, the wonder, the fear, and the delight. Why? Because we've lost God, or at least we've lost our high and lofty concept of God—the only concept of God that He honors.

And so the gains we have made have all been external: Bibles and Bible schools; books and magazines and radio messages; missions and evangelism; numbers and new churches. And the losses we've suffered have all been internal: the loss of dignity and worship and majesty, of inwardness, of God's presence, of fear and spiritual delight.

If we have lost only that which is inward and gained only that which is outward, I wonder if we've gained anything at all. I wonder if we are not now in a bad state. I believe we are. I believe our gospel churches, our Christianity, are thin and anemic, without thoughtful content, frivolous in tone, and worldly in spirit.

And I believe that we are desperately in need of a reformation that will bring the church back. I quit using the word *revival* because we need more than a revival. When the great Welsh revival came to the little country of Wales around the turn of the century, the Holy Ghost had something to work with. The people believed in God and their concept of God was lofty. But because the church has lost her lofty concept of God and no longer knows what God is like, her religion is thin and anemic, frivolous and worldly and cheap.

Compare the preaching of the church today with that of the Hebrew prophets, or even of men like Charles Finney—if you dare to do it. How serious these men of God were! They were men of heaven come to earth to speak to men. As Moses came down from the mount with his face shining to speak to men, so the prophets and preachers down through the years went out. Serious-minded men they were, solemn men, lofty in tone and full of substance of thought and theology.

But today the preaching to a large extent is cheap, frivolous, coarse, shallow, and entertaining. We in the gospel churches think that we've got to entertain the people or they won't come back. We have lost the seriousness out of our preaching and have become silly. We've lost the solemnity and have become fearless. We've lost the loftiness and have become coarse and shallow. We've lost the substance and have become entertainers. This is a tragic and terrible thing.

Compare the Christian reading matter and you'll know that we're in pretty much the same situation. The Germans, the Scots, the Irish, the Welsh, the English, the Americans, and the Canadians all have a common Protestant heritage. And what did they read, these Protestant forebearers of yours and mine? Well, they read Doddridge's *The Rise and Progress of Religion in the Soul.* They read Taylor's *Holy Living and Dying.* They read Bunyan's *Pilgrim's Progress* and *Holy War.* They read Milton's *Paradise Lost.* They read the sermons of John Flavel.

I have an old Methodist hymnal that rolled off the press many years ago, and I found forty-nine hymns on the attributes of God in it. I have heard it said that we shouldn't sing hymns with so much theology because people's minds are different now. We think differently now. Did you know that those Methodist hymns were sung mostly by uneducated people? They were farmers and sheep herders and cattle ranchers, coal miners and blacksmiths, carpenters and cotton pickers—plain people all over this continent. They sang those songs. There are over 1,100 hymns in that hymnbook of mine and there isn't a cheap one in the whole bunch.

And nowadays, I won't even talk about some of the terrible junk that we sing. This tragic and frightening decline in the spiritual state of the churches has come about as a result of our forgetting what kind of God God is. We have lost the vision of the Majesty on high. I have been reading in the book of Ezekiel over the last weeks, reading slowly and rereading, and I've just come to that terrible, frightening, awful passage where the *Shekinah*, the shining presence of God, lifts up from between the wings of the cherubim, goes to the altar, lifts up from the altar, goes to the door, and there is the sound of the whirring of wings (Ezek. 10:4–5). And then the presence of God goes from the door to the outer court (vv. 18–19), and from the outer court to the mountain (Ezek. 11:23), and from the mountain into the glory.

And it has never been back, except as it was incarnated in Jesus Christ when He walked among us. But the *Shekinah* glory that had followed Israel about all those years, that shone over the camp, was gone. God couldn't take it any longer, so He pulled out His Majesty, His *Shekinah* glory, and left the temple. And I wonder how many gospel churches—by their frivolousness, shallowness, coarseness, and worldliness—have grieved the Holy Ghost until He's withdrawn in hurt silence. We must see God again; we must feel God again; we must know God again; we must hear God again. Nothing less than this will save us.

I'm hoping that you will be prayerful and that you'll be worthy to hear this, and that I'll be worthy to speak about God—the triune God, the Father, Son, and Holy Ghost—what He's like. If we can restore again knowledge of God to men, we can help in some small way to bring about a reformation that will

restore God again to men. I want to meditate on these words of
Frederick Faber:

Full of glory, full of wonders, Majesty Divine!
Mid thine everlasting thunders How thy lightnings shine.
Shoreless Ocean! who shall sound Thee?
Thine own eternity is round Thee, Majesty Divine!

One hour with the majesty of God would be worth more to you
now and in eternity than all the preachers—including myself—
that ever stood up to open their Bible. I want a vision of the majesty
of God—not as that song says, "one transient gleam"—no, I don't
want anything transient, I want the gleam of majesty and wonder
to be permanent! I want to live where the face of God shines every
day. No child says, "Mother, let me see your face transiently." The
child wants to be where any minute of the hour he can look up and
see his mother's face.

Timeless, spaceless, single, lonely,
    Yet sublimely Three,
Thou art grandly, always, only
    God in Unity!
Lone in grandeur, lone in glory,
Who shall tell Thy wondrous story,
    Awful Trinity?

Splendours upon splendours beaming
    Change and intertwine;
Glories over glories streaming
    All translucent shine!

Blessings, praises, adorations
Greet Thee from the trembling nations
  Majesty Divine!

This is the day of the common man—and we have not only all become common, but we've dragged God down to our mediocre level. What we need so desperately is an elevated concept of God. Maybe by faithful preaching and prayer, and by the Holy Ghost, we can see the "splendours upon splendours beaming, Change and intertwine." Maybe we can see "Glories over glories streaming, All translucent shine!" To God we can give "blessings, praises, adorations" that "Greet thee from the trembling nations, Majesty Divine!"

EATOR OF HEAVEN AND EARTH; AND IN JESUS CHRI

S   ONLY   SON,   OUR   LO

O   WAS   CONCEIVED   BY   THE   HOLY   SPIR

RN   FROM   THE   VIRGIN   MA

FFERED   UNDER   PONTIUS   PILA

S   CRUCIFIED,   DEAD   AND   BURI

SCENDED   INTO   HELL,   ON   THE   THIRD   [

SE   AGAIN   FROM   THE   DE

CENDED   TO   HEAV

TS   AT   THE   RIGHT   HA

GOD   THE   FATHER   ALMIGH

ENCE   HE   WILL   COME   TO   JUD

E   LIVING   AND   THE   DE

BELIEVE   IN   THE   HOLY   SPIR

E   HOLY   CATHOLIC   CHUR

E   COMMUNION   OF   SAIN

E   REMISSION   OF   SI

E   RESURRECTION   OF   THE   FLE

REATOR OF HEAVEN AND EARTH; AND IN JESUS CHR

IS   ONLY   SON,   OUR   LO

HO   WAS   CONCEIVED   BY   THE   HOLY   SPI

ORN   FROM   THE   VIRGIN   M

UFFERED   UNDER   PONTIUS   PIL

AS   CRUCIFIED,   DEAD   AND   BUR

ESCENDED   INTO   HELL,   ON   THE   THIRD

OSE   AGAIN   FROM   THE   D

SCENDED   TO   HEA

ITS   AT   THE   RIGHT   H

F   GOD   THE   FATHER   ALMIG

HENCE   HE   WILL   COME   TO   JU

HE   LIVING   AND   THE   D

BELIEVE   IN   THE   HOLY   SPI

HE   HOLY   CATHOLIC   CHUR

HE   COMMUNION   OF   SAI

HE   REMISSION   OF   S

HE   RESURRECTION   OF   THE   FL

JESUS CHRIST

And in Jesus Christ his only Son our Lord

We are told that the Word was made flesh. May I point out that within the statement of these few simple words is one of the deepest mysteries of human thought.

Thoughtful men are quick to ask: "How could the deity cross the wide, yawning gulf that separates what is God from that which is not God?" Perhaps you confess with me that in the universe there are really only two things, God and not God—that which is God and that which is not God.

No one could have made God, but God, the Creator, has made all of those things in the universe that are not God.

So, the gulf that separates the Creator and the creature, the gulf between the Being we call God and all other beings, is a great and vast and yawning gulf.

THE MYSTERY OF GOD, MANIFEST IN THE FLESH

How God could bridge this great gulf is indeed one of the most profound and darkest mysteries to which human thought can be directed.

How is it possible that God could join the Creator to the creature? If you do not engage in deep thinking, it may not seem so amazing, but if you have given yourself to frequent thoughtful consideration, you are astonished at the bridging of the great gulf between God and not God.

Let us be reminded that the very archangels and the seraphim and the cherubim who shield the stones of fire are not God.

We read our Bibles and discover that man is not the only order of beings. Man in his sinful pride, however, chooses to believe that he is the only such order.

Some Christian people, and mankind in general, foolishly refuse to believe in the reality of angelic beings. I have talked with enough people to have the feeling that they think of angels as Santa Clauses with wings!

Many say they do not believe in created orders of cherubim and seraphim or watchers or holy ones, or in any of the strange principalities and powers that walk so mysteriously and brightly through the passages of the Bible. Generally speaking, we do not believe in them as much as we should, at any rate.

We may not believe in them, brethren, but they are there! Mankind is only one order of God's beings or creatures. So, we wonder: "How could the Infinite ever become finite? And how could the Limitless One deliberately impose limitations upon

Himself? Why should God favor one order of beings above another in His revelation?"

In the book of Hebrews, we learn to our amazement that God took not upon Him the nature of angels, but He took upon Him the seed of Abraham. Now, Abraham certainly was not equal to an angel. We would suppose that God, in stepping down, would step down just as little as possible. We would think that He would stop with the angels or the seraphim—but instead He came down to the lowest order and took upon Himself the nature of Abraham, the seed of Abraham.

The apostle Paul throws up his hands in wonder at this point. Paul, declared to be one of the six great intellects of all time, throws up his hands and declares that "great is the mystery of godliness" (1 Tim. 3:16), the mystery of God manifest in the flesh.

There are so many more things in heaven and earth than are known in our theology.

Perhaps this is the most becoming approach to the subject for all of us: to just throw up our hands and say, "O Lord, You alone know!" There are so many more things in heaven and earth than are known in our theology—so it is in the deepest sense all mystery.

I would like to quote the gist of what John Wesley said concerning the eternal, mysterious act of God in stooping down to tabernacle with men.

Wesley declared that we should distinguish the act from the method by which the act is performed and advised that we do not reject a fact because we do not know how it was done. I think that is very wise!

I think also that it is very becoming for us to enter into the presence of God reverently, bowing our heads and singing His praises, and acknowledging His loving acts on our behalf even with our words, "It is true, O God, even if we do not know or understand how You have brought it all to pass!"

We will not reject the fact because we do not know the operation that brought it into being.

FULLY GOD, FULLY MAN

How much, then, can we know of this great mystery? We can surely know this, at least: that the incarnation required no compromise of deity. Let us always remember that when God became incarnate there was no compromise on God's part.

In times past, the mythical gods of the nations were no strangers to compromise. The Roman gods, the gods of the Grecian and Scandinavian legends, were gods that could easily compromise themselves and often did in the tales of mythical lore.

But the holy God who is God, and all else not God, our Father who art in heaven, could never compromise Himself. The incarnation, the Word made flesh, was accomplished without any compromise of the Holy Deity.

The living God did not degrade Himself by this condescension. He did not in any sense make Himself to be less than God. He remained ever God and everything else remained not God. The gulf still existed even after Jesus Christ had become man and had dwelt among us. Instead of God degrading Himself when He became man, by the act of incarnation He elevated mankind to Himself.

It is plain in the Athanasian Creed that the early church fathers were cautious at this point of doctrine. They would not allow us to believe that God, in the incarnation, became flesh by a coming down of the Deity into flesh, but rather by the taking up of mankind into God.

The incarnation required no compromise of deity.

Thus, we do not degrade God but we elevate man—and that is the wonder of redemption!

Then, too, there is another thing that we can know for sure about the acts of God—and that is that God can never back out of His bargain. This union of man with God is effected unto perpetuity!

In the sense that we have been considering, God can never cease to be man, for the second person of the Trinity can never un-incarnate Himself, or de-incarnate Himself. The incarnation remains forever a fact, for "the Word was made flesh, and dwelt among us" (John 1:14).

We ought to turn our thoughts here to those earlier days in man's history, for after God had created Adam we know that the Creator communed with men.

I have leafed through a book titled *Earth's Earliest Ages*. I will not say that I have actually read it because I quickly concluded that the author seems to believe that he knows more about the antediluvian period than Moses did. When I discover a man who claims to know more than Moses on a subject in which Moses is a specialist, I shy away from his book.

I admit that I like to dream and dwell in my thoughts upon those ages long past. I have always been fascinated by the Genesis passage that tells us that God came and walked in the garden in the cool of the day, calling for Adam. But Adam was not there. I do not think we are reading anything into the account by assuming that God's meeting with Adam in this way was a common custom at that time. We are not told that this was the first time that God had come to take a walk with Adam in the midst of birdsong and in the fading light.

God and man walked together, and because the Creator had made man in His own image there was no degradation in His communion with man.

But now Adam is in hiding. Pride and disobedience, doubt and failure in testing—sin has broken off the communion and fellowship of the Creator with the created. The holy God must reject the fallen man, sending him from the garden and setting up a flaming sword that he might not return. Adam had lost the presence of the Creator God and in the Bible record of the ages that followed, God never dwelt with men again in quite the same way. The eyes of fallen, sinful men were no longer able to endure the radiant majesty and glory of deity.

Then, in the fullness of time, He came again to men, for "the Word was made flesh, and dwelt among us."

They called His name "Immanuel," which means "God with us." In that first coming of Jesus the Christ, God again came to dwell with men in person.

I will have you know that I am not a prepositional preacher, but at this point we must note three prepositions having to do with the coming of Jesus—God appearing as man.

He appeared to dwell with men. He appeared to be united to men. He came to ultimately dwell in men forever. So, it is with men, and to men, and in men that He came to dwell.

I always note with a little chuckle the frustrations of the translators when they come to such passages as "No man hath seen God at any time, the only begotten Son, which is in the bosom of the Father, he hath declared him" (John 1:18).

God's Word is just too big for the translators. They come to this phrase in the Greek: "The Son hath declared Him." In the English of the King James Version it is just "declared." In other versions they skirt it, they go around it, they plunge through it. They use two or three words and then they come back to one. They do everything to try to say what the Holy Ghost said, but they have to give up. Our English just will not say it all.

When we have used up our words and synonyms, we still have not said all that God revealed when He said: Nobody has ever seen God, but when Jesus Christ came He showed us what God is like (paraphrase of John 1:18).

I suppose that our simple and everyday language is as good as any.

He has revealed Him—He has shown us what God is like! He has declared Him. He has set Him forth. He has revealed Him. In these ways the translators shift their language trying to get at this wondrous miracle of meaning.

But that man walking in Galilee was God acting like God. It was God, limited deliberately, having crossed the wide, mysterious gulf between God and not God; God and creature. No man had seen God at any time.

"The only begotten Son, which is in the bosom of the Father..." (John 1:18)—will you note that *was* is not the tense? Neither does it say that the Son *will be* in the Father's bosom. He *is* in the

41

Father's bosom. It is stated in present, perpetual tense; the continuous tense, I think the grammarians call it. It is the language of continuation.

Therefore, when Jesus hung on the cross, He did not leave the bosom of the Father.

You ask me, then: "Mr. Tozer, if that is true, why did our Lord Jesus cry out, 'My God, my God, why hast thou forsaken me?'" (Mark 15:34).

Was He frightened? Was He mistaken? Never, never!

The answer should be very plain to us who love Him and serve Him.

Even when Christ Jesus died on that unholy, fly-infested cross for mankind, He never divided the Godhead. As the old theologians pointed out, you cannot divide the substance. All of Nero's swords could never cut through the substance of the Godhead to cut off the Father from the Son.

It was Mary's son who cried out, "Why hast thou forsaken me?" It was the human body that God had given Him.

It was the sacrifice that cried, the Lamb about to die.

It was the human Jesus. It was the Son of Man who cried. Believe it that the ancient and timeless Deity was never separated; He was still in the bosom of the Father when He cried, "Into thy hands I commend my spirit" (Luke 23:46).

So the cross did not divide the Godhead—nothing can ever do that. One forever, indivisible, the substance undivided, three persons unconfounded.

Oh, the wonder of the ancient theology of the Christian church! How little we know of it in our day of light-minded shallowness. How much we ought to know of it.

"No man hath seen God at any time, the only begotten Son, which is in the bosom of the Father, he hath declared him" (John 1:18).

CHRIST IN US

God always acts like Himself, wherever He may be and whatever He may be doing; in Him there is neither variableness nor shadow of turning. Yet His infinitude places Him so far above our knowing that a lifetime spent in cultivating the knowledge of Him leaves as much yet to learn as if we had never begun.

God's limitless knowledge and perfect wisdom enable Him to work rationally beyond the bounds of our rational knowing. For this reason, we cannot predict God's actions as we can predict the movements of the heavenly bodies, so He constantly astonishes us as He moves in freedom through His universe. So imperfectly do we know Him that it may be said that one invariable concomitant of a true encounter with God is delighted wonder. No matter how high our expectation may be, when God finally moves into the field of our spiritual awareness we are sure to be astonished by His power to be more wonderful than we anticipate, and more blessed and marvelous than we had imagined He could be.

Yet in a measure His actions may be predicted, for, as I have said, He always acts like Himself. Since we know, for instance, that God is love, we may be perfectly sure that love will be present in His every act, whether it be the salvation of a penitent sinner or the destruction of an impenitent world. Similarly, we can know that He will always be just, faithful, merciful, and true.

It is a rare mind, I suppose, that is much concerned with the conduct of God in those distant realms that lie beyond human experience. But almost everyone has wondered how God would act if He were in our place. And we may have had moments when we felt that God could not possibly understand how hard it is for us to live right in such an evil world as this. And we may have wondered how He would act and what He would do if He were to live among us for a while.

To wonder thus may be natural but it is wholly needless. We know how God would act if He were in our place—*He has been in our place.* It is the mystery of godliness that God was manifest in human flesh. They called His name Immanuel, which being interpreted is *God with us.*

When Jesus walked on earth, He was a man acting like God; but equally wonderful is it that He was also God acting like Himself in a man. We know how God acts in heaven because we saw Him act on earth. "He that hath seen me hath seen the Father; and how sayest thou then, Show us the Father?" (John 14:9).

As glorious as this is, it does not end there. God is still walking in men, and wherever He walks He acts like Himself. This is not poetry but plain, hard fact capable of being tested in the laboratory of life.

That Christ actually inhabits the nature of the regenerate believer is assumed, implied, and overtly stated in the Holy Scriptures. All the Persons of the Godhead are said to enter the nature of the one that engages New Testament truth in faith and obedience. "If a man love me, he will keep my words: and my Father will love him, and we will come unto him, and make our abode with him" (John 14:23). And the doctrine of the indwelling of the Holy Spirit is too well known to need support here; everyone that is taught even slightly in the Word of God understands this.

Whatever God is, the Man Christ Jesus is also. It has been the firm belief of the church from the days of the apostles that God is not only manifest in Christ but that He *is* manifest as Christ. In the days of the Arian controversy, the church fathers were driven to put the teaching of the New Testament on this subject into a highly condensed "rule" or creed which might be accepted as final by all believers. This they did in the following words:

> The right faith is that we believe and confess that our Lord Jesus Christ, the Son of God, is God and Man; God of the substance of His Father, begotten before the worlds; and Man, of the substance of His mother, born in the world. Perfect God and perfect Man, of a reasonable soul and human flesh subsisting.

Christ in a believer's heart will act the same as He acted in Galilee and Judea. His disposition is the same now as then. He was holy, righteous, compassionate, meek, and humble then, and He has not changed. He is the same wherever He is found, whether it be at the right hand of God or in the nature of a true disciple. He was friendly, loving, prayerful, kind, worshipful, self-sacrificing while walking among men; is it not reasonable to expect Him to be the same when walking *in* men?

The church fathers were driven to put the teaching of the New Testament on this subject into a highly condensed "rule" or creed which might be accepted as final by all believers.

Why then do true Christians sometimes act in an un-Christlike manner? Some would assume that when a professed Christian fails to show forth the moral beauty of Christ in his life it is a proof that he has been deceived and is actually not a real Christian at all. But the explanation is not so simple as that.

The truth is that while Christ dwells in the believer's new nature, He has strong competition from the believer's old nature. The warfare between the old and the new goes on continually in most believers. This is accepted as inevitable, but the New Testament does not so teach. A prayerful study of Romans 6–8 points the way to victory. If Christ is allowed complete sway, He will live in us as He lived in Galilee.

EATOR OF HEAVEN AND EARTH; AND IN JESUS CHRI

S ONLY SON, OUR LO

O WAS CONCEIVED BY THE HOLY SPIR

RN FROM THE VIRGIN MA

FFERED UNDER PONTIUS PILA

S CRUCIFIED, DEAD AND BURI

SCENDED INTO HELL, ON THE THIRD

SE AGAIN FROM THE DE

CENDED TO HEAV

TS AT THE RIGHT HA

GOD THE FATHER ALMIGH

ENCE HE WILL COME TO JU

E LIVING AND THE DE

BELIEVE IN THE HOLY SPIR

E HOLY CATHOLIC CHUR

E COMMUNION OF SAIN

E REMISSION OF SI

E RESURRECTION OF THE FLE

EATOR OF HEAVEN AND EARTH; AND IN JESUS CHR

S   ONLY   SON,   OUR   LO

HO   WAS   CONCEIVED   BY   THE   HOLY   SPIR

RN   FROM   THE   VIRGIN   MA

FFERED   UNDER   PONTIUS   PILA

S   CRUCIFIED,   DEAD   AND   BURI

SCENDED   INTO   HELL,   ON   THE   THIRD

SE   AGAIN   FROM   THE   DE

CENDED   TO   HEAV

TS   AT   THE   RIGHT   HA

GOD   THE   FATHER   ALMIGH

ENCE   HE   WILL   COME   TO   JUD

E   LIVING   AND   THE   DE

BELIEVE   IN   THE   HOLY   SPIR

E   HOLY   CATHOLIC   CHUR

E   COMMUNION   OF   SAIN

E   REMISSION   OF   SI

E   RESURRECTION   OF   THE   FLE

3

HOLY SPIRIT

Who was conceived by the Holy Ghost, Born of the Virgin Mary

Neglecting or denying the deity of Christ, the liberals have committed a tragic blunder, for it leaves them nothing but an imperfect Christ whose death was a mere martyrdom and whose resurrection is a myth. They who follow a merely human savior follow no savior at all, but an ideal only, and one furthermore that can do no more than mock their weaknesses and sins. If Mary's Son was not the Son of God in a sense no other man is, then there can be no more hope for the human race. If He who called Himself the light of the world was only a flickering torch, then the darkness that enshrouds the earth is here to stay. So-called Christian leaders shrug this off, but their responsibility toward the souls of their flocks cannot be dismissed with a shrug. God will yet bring them to account for the injury they have done to the people who trusted them as spiritual guides.

But however culpable the act of the liberal in denying the God-hood of Christ, we who pride ourselves on our orthodoxy must not allow our indignation to blind us to our own shortcomings. Certainly this is no time for self-congratulations, for we, too, have in recent years committed a costly blunder in religion, a blunder paralleling closely that of the liberal. Our blunder (or shall we frankly say our sin?) has been to neglect the doctrine of the Spirit to a point where we virtually deny Him His place in the Godhead. This denial has not been by open doctrinal statement, for we have clung closely enough to the biblical position wherever our credal pronouncements are concerned. Our formal creed is sound; *the breakdown is in our working creed.*

This is not a trifling distinction. A doctrine has practical value only as far as it is prominent in our thoughts and makes a differ-ence in our lives. By this test the doctrine of the Holy Spirit as held by evangelical Christians today has almost no practical value at all. In most Christian churches the Spirit is quite entirely over-looked. Whether He is present or absent makes no real difference to anyone. Brief reference is made to Him in the doxology and the benediction. Further than that He might as well not exist. So completely do we ignore Him that it is only by courtesy that we can be called Trinitarian. The Christian doctrine of the Trinity boldly declares the equality of the Three Persons and the right of the Holy Spirit to be worshiped and glorified. Anything less than this is something less than Trinitarianism.

OUR NEGLECT OF THE HOLY SPIRIT

Our neglect of the doctrine of the blessed Third Person has had and is having serious consequences. For doctrine is dynamite. It must have emphasis sufficiently sharp to detonate it before its power is released. Failing this, it may lie quiescent in the back of our minds for the whole of our lives without effect. The doctrine of the Spirit is buried dynamite. Its power awaits discovery and use by the church. The power of the Spirit will not be given to any mincing asset to pneumatological truth. The Holy Spirit cares not at all whether we write Him into our creeds in the back of our hymnals; He awaits our *emphasis*. When He gets into the thinking of the teachers, He will get into the expectation of the hearers. When the Holy Spirit ceases to be incidental and again becomes fundamental, the power of the Spirit will be asserted once more among the people called Christians.

The idea of the Spirit held by the average church member is so vague as to be nearly nonexistent. When he thinks of the matter at all, he is likely to try to imagine a nebulous substance like a wisp of invisible smoke which is said to be present in churches and to hover over good people when they are dying. Frankly he does not believe in any such thing, but he wants to believe something, and not feeling up to the task of examining the whole truth in the light of Scripture he compromises by holding belief in the Spirit as far out from the center of his life as possible, letting it make no difference in anything that touches him practically. This describes a surprisingly large number of earnest persons who are sincerely trying to be Christians.

Now, how should we think of the Spirit? A full answer might well run to a dozen volumes. We can at best only point to the "gracious unction from above" and hope that the reader's own desire may provide the necessary stimulus to urge him on to know the blessed Third Person for himself.

If I read aright the record of Christian experience through the years, those who most enjoyed the power of the Spirit have had the least to say about Him by way of attempted definition. The Bible saints who walked in the Spirit never tried to explain Him. In postbiblical times, many who were filled and possessed by the Spirit were by the limitations of their literary gifts prevented from telling us much about Him. They had no gifts for self-analysis but lived from within in uncritical simplicity. To them the Spirit was One to be loved and fellowshiped the same as the Lord Jesus Himself. They would have been lost completely in any metaphysical discussion of the nature of the Spirit, but they had no trouble in claiming the power of the Spirit for holy living and fruitful service.

This is as it should be. Personal experience must always be first in real life. The most important thing is that we experience reality by the shortest and most direct method. A child may eat nutritious food without knowing anything about the chemistry or dietetics. A country boy may know the delights of pure love while never having heard of Sigmund Freud or Havelock Ellis. Knowledge by acquaintance is always better than mere knowledge by description, and the first does not presuppose the second nor require it.

In religion more than in any other field of human experience a sharp distinction must always be made between *knowing about* and *knowing.* The distinction is the same as between knowing about food and actually eating it. A man can die of starvation knowing all about bread, and a man can remain spiritually dead while knowing all the historic facts of Christianity. "This is life eternal, that they might know thee the only true God, and Jesus Christ, whom thou hast sent" (John 17:3). We have but to introduce one extra word into this verse to see how vast is the difference between knowing about and knowing. "This is life eternal, that they might know *about* thee the only true God, and Jesus Christ, whom thou hast sent." That one word makes all the difference between life and death, for it goes to the very root of the verse and changes its theology radically and vitally.

> *A sharp distinction must always be made between* knowing about *and* knowing.

For all this we would not underestimate the importance of mere knowing about. Its value lies in its ability to rouse us to desire to know in actual experience. Thus knowledge by description may lead on to knowledge by acquaintance. *May* lead on, I say, but does not necessarily do so. Thus we dare not conclude that because we learn about the Spirit we for that reason actually know Him. Knowing Him comes only by a personal encounter with the Holy Spirit Himself.

How shall we think of the Spirit? A great deal can be learned about the Holy Spirit from the word *spirit* itself. Spirit means existence on a level above and beyond matter; it means life subsisting in another mode. Spirit is substance that has no weight, no dimension, no size nor extension in space. These qualities belong to matter and can have no application to spirit. Yet spirit has true being and is objectively real. If this is hard to visualize, just pass it up, for it is at best but a clumsy attempt of the mind to grasp that which is above the mind's powers. And no harm is done if in our thinking about the Spirit we are forced by the limitations of our intellects to clothe Him in the familiar habiliments of material form.

THE ESSENCE OF THE HOLY SPIRIT

How shall we think of the Spirit? The Bible and Christian theology agree to teach that He is a Person, endowed with every quality of personality, such as emotion, intellect, and will. He knows, He wills, He loves; He feels affection, antipathy, and compassion. He thinks, sees, hears, and speaks and performs any act of which personality is capable.

One quality belonging to the Holy Spirit, of great interest and importance to every seeking heart, is penetrability. He can penetrate mind; He can penetrate another spirit, such as the human spirit. He can achieve complete penetration of and actual intermingling with the human spirit. He can invade the human heart and make room for Himself without expelling anything essentially human. The integrity of the human personality remains unimpaired. Only moral evil is forced to withdraw.

The metaphysical problem involved here can no more be avoided than it can be solved. How can one personality enter another? The candid reply would be simply that we do not know, but a near approach to an understanding may be made by a simple analogy borrowed from the old devotional writers of several hundred years ago. We place a piece of iron in a fire and blow up the coals. At first, we have two distinct substances, iron and fire. When we insert the iron in the fire, we achieve the penetration of the iron and we have not only the iron in the fire but the fire in the iron as well. They are two distinct substances, but they have comingled and interpenetrated to a point where the two have become one.

In some such manner does the Holy Spirit penetrate our spirits. In the whole experience we remain our very selves. There is no destruction of substance. Each remains a separate being as before; the difference is that now the Spirit penetrates and fills our personalities, and we are *experientially one with God.*

> *The Apostles' Creed witnesses to faith in the Father and in the Son and in the Holy Ghost and makes no difference between the three.*

How shall we think of the Holy Spirit? The Bible declares that He is God. Every quality belonging to Almighty God is freely attributed to Him. All that God is, the Spirit is declared to be. The Spirit of God is one with and equal to God just as the spirit of a man is equal to and one with the man. This is so fully taught in the Scriptures that we may without loss to the argument omit the formality of proof texts. The most casual reader will have discovered it for himself.

The historic church, when she formulated her "rule of faith," boldly wrote into her confession her belief in the Godhood of the Holy Ghost. The Apostles' Creed witnesses to faith in the Father and in the Son and in the Holy Ghost and makes no difference between the three. The fathers who composed the Nicene Creed testified in a passage of great beauty to their faith in the deity of the Spirit:

And I believe in the Holy Ghost, the Lord and Giver of life,
who proceedeth from the Father and the Son; who with the
Father and the Son together is worshiped and glorified.

The Arian controversy of the fourth century compelled the
fathers to state their beliefs with greater clarity than before.
Among the important writings which appeared at the time is the
Athanasian Creed. Who composed it matters little to us now.
It was written as an attempt to state in as few words as possible
what the Bible teaches about the nature of God; and this it has
done with a comprehensiveness and precision hardly matched
anywhere in the literature of the world. Here are a few quotations
bearing on the deity of the Holy Ghost:

> There is one Person of the Father, another of the Son, and
> another of the Holy Ghost.
>
> But the Godhead of the Father, of the Son, and of the Holy
> Ghost, is all one: the Glory equal, the Majesty coeternal.
>
> And in this Trinity none is afore, or after other: none is
> greater, or less than another;
>
> But the whole three Persons are coeternal together: and
> coequal.
>
> So that in all things, as is aforesaid: the Unity in Trinity, and
> Trinity in Unity is to be worshiped.

In her sacred hymnody, the church has freely acknowledged
the Godhead of the Spirit and in her inspired song she has worshiped Him with joyous abandon. Some of our hymns to the
Spirit have become so familiar that we tend to miss their true

meaning by the very circumstances of their familiarity. Such a hymn is the wondrous "Holy Ghost, with Light Divine"; another is the more recent "Breathe on Me, Breath of God"; and there are many others. They have been sung so often by persons who have had no experiential knowledge of their content that for most of us they have become almost meaningless.

In the poetical works of Frederick Faber I have found a hymn to the Holy Spirit which I would rank among the finest ever written, but so far as I know it has not been set to music, or if it has, it is not sung today in any church with which I am acquainted. Could the reason be that it embodies a personal experience of the Holy Spirit so deep, so intimate, so fiery hot that it corresponds to nothing in the hearts of the worshipers in present-day evangelicalism? I quote three stanzas:

Fountain of Love!
Thyself true God!
Who through eternal days
From Father and from Son
hast flowed in uncreated ways!

I dread Thee, Unbegotten Love!
True God! sole Fount of Grace!
And now before Thy blessed throne
My sinful self abase.

O Light! O Love! O very God
I dare no longer gaze
Upon Thy wondrous attributes
And their mysterious ways.

These lines have everything to make a great hymn: sound theology, smooth structure, lyric beauty, high compression of profound ideas, and a full charge of lofty religious feeling. Yet they are in complete neglect. I believe that a mighty resurgence of the Spirit's power among us will open again wells of hymnody long forgotten. For song can never bring the Holy Spirit, but the Holy Spirit does invariably bring song.

What we have in the Christian doctrine of the Holy Spirit is Deity present among us. He is not God's messenger only; *He is God.* He is God in contact with His creatures, doing in them and among them a saving and renewing work.

The persons of the Godhead never work separately. We dare not think of them in such a way as to "divide the substance." Every act of God is done by all three persons. God is never anywhere present in one person without the other two. He cannot divide Himself. Where the Spirit is, there also is the Father and the Son. "We will come unto him, and make our abode with him" (John 14:23). For the accomplishment of some specific work one person may for the time be more prominent than the others are, but never is He alone. God is altogether present wherever He is present at all.

To the reverent question, "What is God like?" a proper answer will always be, "He is like Christ." For Christ is God, and the Man who walked among men in Palestine was God acting like Himself in the familiar situation where His incarnation placed Him. To the question, "What is the Spirit like?" the answer must always be, "He is like Christ." For the Spirit is the essence of the Father and the Son. As they are, so is He. As we feel toward Christ and toward our Father who art in heaven, so should we feel toward the Spirit of the Father and the Son.

The Holy Spirit is the Spirit of life and light and love. In His uncreated nature He is a boundless sea of fire, flowing, moving ever, performing as He moves the eternal purposes of God. Toward nature He performs one sort of work, toward the world another, and toward the church still another. And every act of His accords with the will of the triune God. Never does He act on impulse nor move after a quick or arbitrary decision. Since He is the Spirit of the Father, He feels toward His people exactly as the Father feels, so there need be on our part no sense of strangeness in His presence. He will always act like Jesus, toward sinners in compassion, toward saints in warm affection, toward human suffering in tenderest pity and love.

REPENTING FOR OUR NEGLECT

It is time for us to repent, for our transgressions against the blessed Third Person have been many and much aggravated. We have bitterly mistreated Him in the house of His friends. We have crucified Him in His own temple as they crucified the Eternal Son on the hill above Jerusalem. And the nails we used were not of iron, but of finer and more precious stuff of which human life is made. Out of our hearts we took the refined metals of will and feeling and thought, and from them we fashioned the nails of suspicion and rebellion and neglect. By unworthy thoughts about Him and unfriendly attitudes toward Him we grieved and quenched Him days without end.

The truest and most acceptable repentance is to reverse the acts and attitudes of which we repent. A thousand years of remorse over a wrong act would not please God as much as a change of conduct and a reformed life. "Let the wicked forsake his way, and the unrighteous man his thoughts: and let him return unto the Lord, and he will have mercy upon him; and to our God, for he will abundantly pardon" (Isa. 55:7).

We can best repent our neglect by neglecting Him no more. Let us begin to think of Him as One to be worshiped and obeyed. Let us throw open every door and invite Him in. Let us surrender to Him every room in the temple of our hearts and insist that He enter and occupy as Lord and Master within His own dwelling. And let us remember that He is drawn to the sweet name of Jesus as bees are drawn to the fragrance of clover. Where Christ is honored the Spirit is sure to feel welcome; where Christ is glorified He will move about freely, pleased and at home.

EATOR OF HEAVEN AND EARTH; AND IN JESUS CHRI

S   ONLY   SON,   OUR   LO

O   WAS   CONCEIVED   BY   THE   HOLY   SPIR

RN   FROM   THE   VIRGIN   MA

FFERED   UNDER   PONTIUS   PILA

S   CRUCIFIED,   DEAD   AND   BURI

SCENDED   INTO   HELL,   ON   THE   THIRD

SE   AGAIN   FROM   THE   DE

CENDED   TO   HEAV

TS   AT   THE   RIGHT   HA

GOD   THE   FATHER   ALMIGH

ENCE   HE   WILL   COME   TO   JU

E   LIVING   AND   THE   DE

BELIEVE   IN   THE   HOLY   SPIR

E   HOLY   CATHOLIC   CHUR

E   COMMUNION   OF   SAIN

E   REMISSION   OF   SI

E   RESURRECTION   OF   THE   FLE

REATOR OF HEAVEN AND EARTH; AND IN JESUS CHR

IS   ONLY   SON,   OUR   LO

HO   WAS   CONCEIVED   BY   THE   HOLY   SPI

ORN   FROM   THE   VIRGIN   MA

UFFERED   UNDER   PONTIUS   PILA

AS   CRUCIFIED,   DEAD   AND   BUR

ESCENDED   INTO   HELL,   ON   THE   THIRD

OSE   AGAIN   FROM   THE   DE

SCENDED   TO   '   HEAV

TS   AT   THE   RIGHT   H

F   GOD   THE   FATHER   ALMIGH

ENCE   HE   WILL   COME   TO   JU

E   LIVING   AND   THE   DE

E   BELIEVE   IN   THE   HOLY   SPI

E   HOLY   CATHOLIC   CHUR

E   COMMUNION   OF   SAIN

E   REMISSION   OF   SI

E   RESURRECTION   OF   THE   FLE

4

CRUCIFIED

Suffered under Pontius Pilate, was crucified, dead, and buried:
He descended into hell

There is a strange conspiracy of silence in the world today—even in religious circles—about man's responsibility for sin, the reality of judgment, and about an outraged God and the necessity for a crucified Savior.

On the other hand, there is an open and powerful movement swirling throughout the world designed to give people peace of mind in relieving them of any historical responsibility for the trial and crucifixion of Jesus Christ. The problem with modern decrees and pronouncements in the name of brotherhood and tolerance is their basic misconception of Christian theology.

A great shadow lies upon every man and every woman—the fact that our Lord was bruised and wounded and crucified for the entire human race. This is the basic human responsibility that men are trying to push off and evade.

Let us not eloquently blame Judas nor Pilate. Let us not curl our lips at Judas and accuse, "He sold Him for money!"

Let us pity Pilate, the weak-willed, because he did not have courage enough to stand for the innocence of the man whom he declared had done no wrong.

Let us not curse the Jews for delivering Jesus to be crucified. Let us not single out the Romans in blaming them for putting Jesus on the cross.

Oh, they were guilty, certainly! But they were our accomplices in crime. They and we put Him on the cross, not they alone. That rising malice and anger that burns so hotly in your being today put Him there. That basic dishonesty that comes to light in your being when you knowingly cheat and chisel on your income tax return—that put Him on the cross. The evil, the hatred, the suspicion, the jealousy, the lying tongue, the carnality, the fleshly love of pleasure—all of these in natural man joined in putting Him on the cross.

OUR RESPONSIBILITY

We put Him there. We may as well admit it. Every one of us in Adam's race had a share in putting Him on the cross!

I have often wondered how any professing Christian man or woman could approach the Communion table and participate in the memorial of our Lord's death without feeling and sensing the pain and the shame of the inward confession: "I, too, am among those who helped put Him on the cross!"

I remind you that it is characteristic of the natural man to keep himself so busy with unimportant trifles that he is able to avoid the settling of the most important matters relating to life and existence.

Men and women will gather anywhere and everywhere to talk about and discuss every subject from the latest fashions on up to Plato and philosophy—up and down the scale. They talk about the necessity for peace. They may talk about the church and how it can be a bulwark against communism. None of these things are embarrassing subjects.

But the conversation all stops and the taboo of silence becomes effective when anyone dares to suggest that there are spiritual subjects of vital importance to our souls that ought to be discussed and considered. There seems to be an unwritten rule in polite society that if any religious subjects are to be discussed, it must be within the framework of theory—"never let it get personal!"

All the while, there is really only one thing that is of vital and lasting importance—the fact that our Lord Jesus Christ "was wounded for our transgressions, he was bruised for our iniquities: the chastisement of our peace was upon him; and with his stripes we are healed" (Isa. 53:5).

There are two very strong and terrible words here—*transgressions* and *iniquities*.

A *transgression* is a breaking away, a revolt from just authority. In all of the moral universe, only man and the fallen angels have rebelled and violated the authority of God, and men are still in flagrant rebellion against that authority.

There is no expression in the English language which can convey the full weight and force of terror inherent in the words *transgression* and *iniquity*. But in man's fall and transgression against the created order and authority of God we recognize perversion and twistedness and deformity and crookedness and rebellion. These are all there, and, undeniably, they reflect the reason and the necessity for the death of Jesus Christ on the cross.

The word *iniquity* is not a good word—and God knows how we hate it! But the consequences of iniquity cannot be escaped. The prophet reminds us clearly that the Savior was bruised for "our iniquities."

We deny it and say, "No!" but the fingerprints of all mankind are plain evidence against us. The authorities have no trouble finding and apprehending the awkward burglar who leaves his fingerprints on tables and doorknobs, for they have his record. So, the fingerprints of man are found in every dark cellar and in every alley and in every dimly lighted evil place throughout the world—every man's fingerprints are recorded, and God knows man from man. It is impossible to escape our guilt and place our moral responsibilities upon someone else. It is a highly personal matter—"our iniquities."

IMPLICATIONS OF THE CRUCIFIXION

For our iniquities and our transgressions He was bruised and wounded. I do not even like to tell you of the implications of His wounding. It really means that He was profaned and broken, stained and defiled. He was Jesus Christ when men took Him into their evil hands. Soon He was humiliated and profaned. They plucked out His beard. He was stained with His own blood, defiled with earth's grime. Yet He accused no one and He cursed no one. He was Jesus Christ, the wounded One.

Israel's great burden and amazing blunder was her judgment that this wounded one on the hillside beyond Jerusalem was being punished for His own sin.

Isaiah foresaw this historic error in judgment, and he himself was a Jew, saying: "We thought He was smitten of God. We thought that God was punishing Him for His own iniquity for we did not know then that God was punishing Him for our transgressions and our iniquities." He was profaned for our sakes. He who is the second person of the Godhead was not only wounded for us, but He was also profaned by ignorant and unworthy men.

Isaiah reported that "the chastisement of our peace was upon him." How few there are who realize that it is this peace—the health and prosperity and welfare and safety of the individual—which restores us to God. A chastisement fell upon Him so that we as individual humans could experience peace with God if we so desired. But the chastisement was upon Him. Rebuke, discipline, and correction—these are found in chastisement. He was beaten and scourged in public by the decree of the Romans. They lashed Him in public view as they later lashed Paul. They whipped and punished Him in full view of the jeering public, and His bruised and bleeding and swollen person was the answer to the peace of the world and to the peace of the human heart. He was chastised for our peace; the blows fell upon Him.

I do not suppose there is any more humiliating punishment ever devised by mankind than that of whipping and flogging grown men in public view. Many men who have been put in a jail have become a kind of hero in the eye of the public. Heavy fines have been assessed against various offenders of the law, but it is not unusual for such an offender to boast and brag about his escape. But when a bad man is taken out before a laughing, jeering crowd, stripped to the waist and soundly whipped like a child—a bad child—he loses face and has no boasting left. He will probably never be the bold, bad man he was before. That kind of whipping and chastisement breaks the spirit and humiliates. The chagrin is worse than the lash that falls on the back.

I speak for myself as a forgiven and justified sinner, and I think I speak for a great host of forgiven and born-again men and women, when I say that in our repentance we sensed just a fraction and just a token of the wounding and chastisement which fell upon Jesus Christ as He stood in our place and in our behalf. A truly penitent man who has realized the enormity of his sin and rebellion against God senses a violent revulsion against himself—he does not feel that he can actually dare to ask God to let him off. But peace has been established, for the blows have fallen on Jesus Christ. He was publicly humiliated and disgraced as a common thief, wounded and bruised and bleeding under the lash for sins He did not commit, for rebellions in which He had no part, for iniquity in the human stream that was an outrage to a loving God and Creator.

SIGNIFICANCE OF THE CRUCIFIXION

Isaiah sums up his message of a substitutionary atonement with the good news that "with his stripes we are healed."

The meaning of these "stripes" in the original language is not a pleasant description. It means to be actually hurt and injured until the entire body is black and blue as one great bruise. Mankind has always used this kind of bodily laceration as a punitive measure. Society has always insisted upon the right to punish a man for his own wrongdoing. The punishment is generally suited to the nature of the crime. It is a kind of revenge—society taking vengeance against the person who dared flout the rules.

But the suffering of Jesus Christ was not punitive. It was not for Himself and not for punishment of anything that He Himself had done.

The suffering of Jesus was corrective. He was willing to suffer in order that He might correct us and perfect us, so that His suffering might not begin and end in suffering, but that it might begin in suffering and end in healing.

Brethren, that is the glory of the cross! That is the glory of the kind of sacrifice that was for so long in the heart of God! That is the glory of the kind of atonement that allows a repentant sinner to come into peaceful and gracious fellowship with his God and Creator! It began in His suffering and it ended in our healing. It began in His wounds and ended in our purification. It began in His bruises and ended in our cleansing.

What is our repentance? I discover that repentance is mainly remorse for the share we had in the revolt that wounded Jesus Christ, our Lord. Further, I have discovered that truly repentant men never quite get over it, for repentance is not a state of mind and spirit that takes its leave as soon as God has given forgiveness and as soon as cleansing is realized.

That painful and acute conviction that accompanies repentance may well subside and a sense of peace and cleansing come, but even the holiest of justified men will think back over his part in the wounding and the chastisement of the Lamb of God. A sense of shock will still come over him. A sense of wonder will remain— wonder that the Lamb that was wounded should turn His wounds into the cleansing and forgiveness of one who wounded Him.

This brings to mind a gracious moving in many of our evangelical church circles—a willingness to move toward the spiritual purity of heart taught and exemplified so well by John Wesley in a time of spiritual dryness.

In spite of the fact that the word *sanctification* is a good Bible word, we have experienced a period in which evangelical churches hardly dared breathe the word because of the fear of being classified among the "holy rollers."

Not only is the good word *sanctification* coming back, but I am hopeful that what the word stands for in the heart and mind of God is coming back too. The believing Christian, the child of God, should have a holy longing and desire for the pure heart and clean hands that are a delight to his Lord. It was for this that Jesus Christ allowed Himself to be humiliated, maltreated, lacerated. He was bruised, wounded, and chastised so that the people of God could be a cleansed and spiritual people—in order that our minds might be pure and our thoughts pure. This provision all began in His suffering and ends in our cleansing. It began with His open, bleeding wounds and ends in peaceful hearts and calm and joyful demeanor in His people.

OUR AMAZEMENT AND WONDER

Every humble and devoted believer in Jesus Christ must have his own periods of wonder and amazement at this mystery of godliness—the willingness of the Son of Man to take our place in judgment and in punishment. If the amazement has all gone out of it, something is wrong, and you need to have the stony ground broken up again!

I often remind you that Paul, one of the holiest men who ever lived, was not ashamed of his times of remembrance and wonder over the grace and kindness of God. He knew that God did not hold his old sins against him forever. Knowing the account was all settled, Paul's happy heart assured him again and again that all was well. At the same time, Paul could only shake his head in amazement, and confess: "I am unworthy to be called, but by His grace, I am a new creation in Jesus Christ!"

I make this point about the faith and assurance and rejoicing of Paul in order to say that if that humble sense of perpetual penance ever leaves our justified being, we are on the way to backsliding.

Charles Finney, one of the greatest of all of God's men throughout the years, testified that in the midst of his labors and endeavors in bringing men to Christ, he would at times sense a coldness in his own heart.

Finney did not excuse it. In his writings he told of having to turn from all of his activities, seeking God's face and Spirit anew in fasting and prayer. "I plowed up until I struck fire and met God," he wrote. What a helpful and blessed formula for the concerned children of God in every generation!

Those who compose the body of Christ, His church, must be inwardly aware of two basic facts if we are to be joyfully effective for our Lord. We must have the positive knowledge that we are clean through His wounds, with God's peace realized through His stripes. This is how God assures us that we may be all right inside. In this spiritual condition, we will treasure the purity of His cleansing and we will not excuse any evil or wrongdoing. Also, we must keep upon us a joyful and compelling sense of gratitude for the bruised and wounded One, our Lord Jesus Christ. Oh, what a mystery of redemption—that the bruises of One healed the bruises of many; that the wounds of One healed the wounds of millions; that the stripes of One healed the stripes of many.

The wounds and bruises that should have fallen upon us fell upon Him, and we are saved for His sake!

Many years ago, an historic group of Presbyterians were awed by the wonder and the mystery of Christ's having come in the flesh to give Himself as an offering for every man's sin.

Those humble Christians said to one another: "Let us walk softly and search our hearts and wait on God and seek His face throughout the next three months. Then we will come to the Communion table with our hearts prepared—lest the table of our Lord should become a common and careless thing." God still seeks humble, cleansed, and trusting hearts through which to reveal His divine power and grace and life. A professional botanist from the university can describe the acacia bush of the desert better than Moses could ever do—but God is still looking for the humble souls who are not satisfied until God speaks with the divine fire in the bush.

A research scientist could be employed to stand and tell us more about the elements and properties found in bread and wine than the apostles ever knew. But this is our danger: we may have lost the light and warmth of the presence of God, and we may have only bread and wine. The fire will have gone from the bush, and the glory will not be in our act of communion and fellowship.

It is not so important that we know all of the history and all of the scientific facts, but it is vastly important that we desire and know and cherish the presence of the Living God, who has given "Jesus Christ the righteous: And he is the propitiation for our sins: and not for ours only, but also for the sins of the whole world" (1 John 2:1–2).

A NOTE ABOUT CHRIST DESCENDING INTO HELL

I am going to add a word about Christ descending into hell and preaching to the spirits in prison. Though the meaning of these phrases may be obscure, I am not going to pass it by for a number of reasons. First, we have all Bible passages by divine inspiration, even the obscure ones. If our Lord did not intend for us to expound it, He would not have put it here. Obscure passages need to be treated with respect, even if we do not yet fully understand.

Second, I want people to be fully informed. We cannot be informed if we skip the hard places, and major only in the Scriptures that can be understood.

Third—the most important reason—false teachers specialize in difficult texts. Heresy always thrives in obscurity, or in obscure passages. Heresy dies when the full light of God reaches it.

If I were to take you to a farm, I could say to you, "Now here you will find apples, peaches, and grapes. And here are watermelons, and cantaloupes, and sweet potatoes." I could name fifteen or twenty edible fruits or vegetables or grains and say, "Now this is all yours. Take over—*work*."

What if I came back a month later and found my guests half starved? I would say to them, "What's the matter? You look undernourished."

They might reply, "Well, we are undernourished because we found a plant that we can't identify. There is a plant behind the old oak stump back there near the end of the far field just over the hill. And we have spent one month trying to identify this plant."

And that's exactly what a lot of God's children do. They starve themselves to death, knee deep in clover, because there's one little plant at the rear end of the field that they can't identify. Heretics always starve you to death while worrying about one obscure passage of Scripture.

You will remember the Apostles' Creed, which our church used to quote sometimes (then we sort of quit). We all believe the Apostles' Creed, and what it says about our Lord,

Who was conceived by the Holy Ghost,
Born of the Virgin Mary: Suffered under Pontius Pilate,
Was crucified, dead, and buried:
The third day he rose again from the dead.

Now that's the way we Protestants have quoted it. But the old Apostles' Creed reads like this:

Who was conceived by the Holy Ghost,
Born of the Virgin Mary: Suffered under Pontius Pilate,
Was crucified, dead, and buried:
He descended into hell;
The third day he rose again from the dead.

Now the old Creed was only saying what was said in 1 Peter 3:18–20:

> For Christ also hath once suffered for sins, the just for the unjust, that he might bring us to God, being put to death in the flesh, but quickened by the Spirit: By which also he went and preached unto the spirits in prison; Which sometime were disobedient, when once the longsuffering of God waited in the days of Noah, while the ark was a preparing, wherein few, that is, eight souls were saved by water.

The Scriptures spoke of "spirits in prison," and at least some of these are identified as being the disobedient part of the earth's population at the time of Noah's flood. They heard the message Noah preached, and they denied or rejected it, and they perished along with their evil deeds at the coming of the flood. This passage teaches us that the "disobedient" all went to the place of the dead, called *Hades* in the New Testament and *Sheol* in the Old Testament.

At the crucifixion, when Jesus Christ's spirit was free from the crucified body, His Spirit did not hover over the tomb. The eternal Son—in His Spirit—had a work to do. When He "descended into hell," He did not descend into *the fires of hell for punishment*, but He descended to *the place of the dead*. There He preached the Word to those who had died, whose spirits were confined there.

The crucified Christ told them that judgment had come, and He justified the ways of God to man, explaining what had taken place so they might know that they were being treated as intelligent, moral beings. Our Lord went to them in His Spirit and preached to them and explained how things were, so that justice might be done.

Something like this goes on in ordinary English or American courts. The evidence has been heard, the jury goes out and deliberates, and they pronounce the defendant guilty. The judge says, "Will the defendant please rise and face the court?" The defendant rises. And the judge says something to this effect: "All the evidence has been heard, and a jury of your peers has decided from the evidence that you have been guilty of this crime. Before you are sentenced, is there anything you want to say?"

In other words, we're about to sentence you and we want to clear this whole matter up. Have you anything to say? Usually the defendant doesn't say anything, but if there was anything, the judge would give it respectful consideration.

So God says all the wicked were swept away as by a flood, hurled to the place of the dead, and they will never see the blessedness of heaven. But they are human, they are moral creatures. They are capable of exercising judgment on their own right. Therefore, the everlasting Son of God went before the spirits in prison and preached to them as though they were living. They were alive in their spirit—they had sinned in the flesh. And they were to be judged for the days they lived in the flesh.

He preached deliverance to the ransomed and judgment to the lost. He took His ransomed ones with Him, and He left the lost for the final judgment. Everyone—those under the earth, and those on the earth, and all creatures everywhere—will admit that "Jesus Christ is Lord, to the glory of God the Father (Phil. 2:11).

We need to understand obscure Scripture passages, even if

they don't bless us at the time. We need a shield of truth to raise against the fiery darts of error. With bowed heads and reverent minds, we receive the hard and obscure things as well as the easy things of Scripture.

REATOR OF HEAVEN AND EARTH; AND IN JESUS CHR

IS ONLY SON, OUR LO

HO WAS CONCEIVED BY THE HOLY SPI

ORN FROM THE VIRGIN MA

FFERED UNDER PONTIUS PILA

AS CRUCIFIED, DEAD AND BURI

SCENDED INTO HELL, ON THE THIRD

SE AGAIN FROM THE DE

CENDED TO HEAV

TS AT THE RIGHT HA

GOD THE FATHER ALMIGH

ENCE HE WILL COME TO JU

E LIVING AND THE DE

BELIEVE IN THE HOLY SPIR

E HOLY CATHOLIC CHUR

E COMMUNION OF SAIN

E REMISSION OF SI

E RESURRECTION OF THE FLE

RESURRECTED AND ASCENDED

The third day he rose again from the dead:
He ascended into heaven, And sitteth on the right hand
of God the Father Almighty

The celebration of Christ's resurrection began very early in the church and has continued without interruption to this day. There is scarcely a church anywhere but will observe Easter in some manner, whether it be by simply singing a resurrection hymn or by the performance of the most elaborate rites.

Ignoring the etymological derivation of the word *Easter* and the controversy that once gathered around the question of the date on which it should be observed, and admitting as we must that to millions the whole thing is little more than a pagan festival, I want to ask and try to answer two questions. The first question is, "What is the resurrection all about?" and the second, "What practical meaning does it have for the plain Christian of today?"

The first may be answered briefly or its answer could run into a thousand pages. The real significance of the day stems from an event, a solid historical incident that took place on a certain day in a geographical location that can be identified on any good map of the world. It was first announced by the two men who stood beside the empty tomb and said simply, "He is not here: for he is risen" (Matt. 28:6), and was later affirmed in the solemnly beautiful words of one who saw Him after His resurrection:

> But now is Christ risen from the dead, and become the firstfruits of them that slept. For since by man came death, by man came also the resurrection of the dead. For as in Adam all die, even so in Christ shall all be made alive. But every man in his own order: Christ the firstfruits; afterward they that are Christ's at his coming. (1 Cor. 15:20–23)

That is what the resurrection is about. The Man called Jesus is alive after having been publicly put to death by crucifixion. The Roman soldiers nailed Him to the cross and watched Him till the life had gone from Him. Then a responsible company of persons, headed by one Joseph of Arimathea, took the body down from the cross and laid it in a tomb, after which the Roman authorities sealed the tomb and set a watch before it to make sure the body would not be stolen away by zealous but misguided disciples. This last precaution was the brainchild of the priests and the Pharisees, and how it backfired on them is known to the ages, for it went far to confirm the fact that the body was completely dead and that it could have gotten out of the tomb only by some miracle.

In spite of the tomb and the watch and the seal, in spite of death itself, the Man who had been laid in the place of death walked out alive after three days. That is the simple historical fact attested by more than five hundred trustworthy persons, among them being a man who is said by some scholars to have had one of the mightiest intellects of all time. That man of course was Saul, who later became a disciple of Jesus and was known as Paul the apostle. This is what the church has believed and celebrated throughout the centuries. This is what the church celebrates today.

Granted that this is all true, what does it or can it mean to us who live so far removed in space from the event and so far away in time? Several thousand miles and nearly two thousand years separate us from that first bright Easter morning. Apart from or in addition to the joy of returning spring and the sweet music and the sense of cheerfulness associated with the day, what practical significance does Easter have for us?

To borrow the words of Paul, "Much every way!" (Rom. 3:2). For one thing, any question about Christ's death was forever cleared away by His resurrection. He was "declared to be the Son of God with power, according to the spirit of holiness, by the resurrection from the dead" (Rom. 1:4). Also, His place in the intricate web of Old Testament prophecy was fully established when He arose. When He walked with the two discouraged disciples after His resurrection, He chided them for their unbelief and then asked, "Ought not Christ to have suffered these things, and to enter into his glory? And beginning at Moses and all the prophets, he expounded unto them in all the scriptures the things concerning himself" (Luke 24:26–27).

Then it should be remembered that He could not save us by the cross alone. He must rise from the dead to give validity to His finished work. A dead Christ would be as helpless as the ones He tried to save. He "was raised again for our justification" (Rom. 4:25), said Paul, and in so saying declared that our hope of righteousness depended upon our Lord's ability to beat death and rise beyond its power.

He could not save us by the cross alone. He must rise from the dead to give validity to His finished work.

It is of great practical importance to us to know that *the Christ who lived again still lives.* "Therefore let all the house of Israel know assuredly, that God hath made the same Jesus, whom ye have crucified, both Lord and Christ" (Acts 2:36), said Peter on the day of Pentecost; and this accorded with our Lord's own words, "All power is given unto me in heaven and in earth" (Matt. 28:18), and with the words of Hebrews, "Now of the things which we have spoken this is the sum: We have such an high priest, who is set on the right hand of the throne of the Majesty in the heavens" (Heb. 8:1).

Not only does He still live, but *He can never die again.* "Knowing that Christ being raised from the dead dieth no more; death hath no more dominion over him" (Rom. 6:9).

Finally, all that Christ is, all that He has accomplished for us is available to us now if we obey and trust.

We are more than conquerors, through our Captain's triumph; let us shout the victory as we onward go.

AT THE FATHER'S RIGHT HAND

At the risk of sounding more than slightly repetitious, I want to urge again that we Christians look again to our doctrinal emphases.

If we would know the power of truth we must emphasize it. Creedal truth is coal lying inert in the depths of the earth waiting release. Dig it out, shovel it into the combustion chamber of some huge engine, and the mighty energy that lay asleep for centuries will create light and heat and cause the machinery of a great factory to surge into productive action. The theory of coal never turned a wheel nor warmed a hearth. Power must be released to be made effective.

In the redemptive work of Christ three major epochs may be noted: His birth, His death, and His subsequent elevation to the right hand of God. These are the three main pillars that uphold the temple of Christianity; upon them rest all the hopes of mankind, world without end. All else that He did takes its meaning from these three Godlike deeds.

It is imperative that we believe all these truths, but the big question is where to lay the emphasis. Which truth should, at a given time, receive the sharpest accent? We are exhorted to look unto Jesus, but where shall we look? Unto Jesus in the manger? on the cross? at the throne? These questions are far from academic. It is of great practical importance to us that we get the right answer.

Of course we must include in our total creed the manger, the cross, and the throne. All that is symbolized by these three objects must be present to the gaze of faith; all is necessary to a proper understanding of the Christian evangel. No single tenet of our creed must be abandoned or even relaxed, for each is joined to the other by a living bond. But while all truth is to be at all times held inviolate, not every truth is to be at all times emphasized equally with every other. Our Lord indicated as much when He spoke of the faithful and wise steward who gave to his master's household "their portion of meat in due season" (Luke 12:42).

We must include in our total creed the manger, the cross, and the throne.

Mary brought forth her firstborn Son and wrapped Him in swaddling clothes and laid Him in a manger. Wise men came to worship, shepherds wondered, and angels chanted of peace and good will toward men. All taken together this scene is so chastely beautiful, so winsome, so tender, that the like of it is not found anywhere in the literature of the world. It is not hard to see why Christians have tended to place such emphasis upon the manger, the meek-eyed virgin, and the Christ child. In certain Christian circles, the major emphasis is made to fall upon the child in the manger. Why this is so is understandable, but the emphasis is nevertheless misplaced. Christ was born that He might become a man and became a man that He might give His life as ransom for many. Neither the birth nor the dying were ends in themselves. As He was born to die, so did He die that He might atone, and rise that He might justify freely all who take refuge in Him. His birth and His death are history. His appearance at the mercy seat is not history past, but a present, continuing fact, to the instructed Christian the most glorious fact his trusting heart can entertain. This Easter season might be a good time to get our emphases corrected. Let us remember that weakness lies at the manger, death at the cross, and power at the throne. Our Christ is not in a manger. Indeed, New Testament theology nowhere presents the Christ child as an object of saving faith. The gospel that stops at the manger is another gospel and no good news at all. The church that still gathers around the manger can only be weak and misty-eyed, mistaking sentimentality for the power of the Holy Spirit.

As there is now no babe in the manger at Bethlehem so there is no man on the cross at Jerusalem. To worship the babe in the manger or the man on the cross is to reverse the redemptive processes of God and turn the clock back on His eternal purposes. Let the church place its major emphasis upon the cross and there can be only pessimism, gloom, and fruitless remorse. Let a sick man die hugging a crucifix and what have we there? Two dead men in a bed, neither of which can help the other.

The glory of the Christian faith is that the Christ who died for our sins rose again for our justification. We should joyfully remember His birth and gratefully muse on His dying, but the crown of all our hopes is with Him at the Father's right hand.

Paul gloried in the cross and refused to preach anything except Christ and Him crucified, but to him the cross stood for the whole redemptive work of Christ. In his epistles Paul writes of the incarnation and the crucifixion, yet he stops not at the manger or the cross but constantly sweeps our thoughts on to the resurrection and upward to the ascension and the throne.

> *We should joyfully remember His birth and gratefully muse on His dying, but the crown of all our hopes is with Him at the Father's right hand.*

"All power is given unto me in heaven and in earth" (Matt. 28:18), said our risen Lord before He went up on high, and the first Christians believed Him and went forth to share His triumph. "And with great power gave the apostles witness of the resurrection of the Lord Jesus: and great grace was upon them all" (Acts 4:33).

Should the church shift her emphasis from the weakness of the manger and the death of the cross to the life and power of the enthroned Christ, perhaps she might recapture her lost glory. It is worth a try.

BELIEVE IN GOD

EATOR OF HEAVEN AND EARTH; AND IN JESUS CHRI

S ONLY SON, OUR LO

O WAS CONCEIVED BY THE HOLY SPIR

RN FROM THE VIRGIN MA

FFERED UNDER PONTIUS PILA

S CRUCIFIED, DEAD AND BURI

SCENDED INTO HELL; ON THE THIRD D

SE AGAIN FROM THE DE

CENDED TO HEAV

TS AT THE RIGHT HA

GOD THE FATHER ALMIGH

ENCE HE WILL COME TO JU

E LIVING AND THE DE

BELIEVE IN THE HOLY SPIR

E HOLY CATHOLIC CHUR

E COMMUNION OF SAIN

E REMISSION OF SI

E RESURRECTION OF THE FLE

REATOR OF HEAVEN AND EARTH; AND IN JESUS CHR

IS   ONLY   SON,   OUR   LO

HO   WAS   CONCEIVED   BY   THE   HOLY   SPI

ORN   FROM   THE   VIRGIN   MA

UFFERED   UNDER   PONTIUS   PILA

AS   CRUCIFIED,   DEAD   AND   BUR

ESCENDED   INTO   HELL,   ON   THE   THIRD

OSE   AGAIN   FROM   THE   DE

CENDED   TO   HEAV

TS   AT   THE   RIGHT   H

F   GOD   THE   FATHER   ALMIGH

ENCE   HE   WILL   COME   TO   JU

E   LIVING   AND   THE   DE

BELIEVE   IN   THE   HOLY   SPI

E   HOLY   CATHOLIC   CHUR

E   COMMUNION   OF   SAIN

E   REMISSION   OF   SI

E   RESURRECTION   OF   THE   FLE

6

RETURNING

From thence he shall come to judge the quick and the dead

Are you ready for the appearing of Jesus Christ, or are you among those who are merely curious about His coming?

Let me warn you that many preachers and Bible teachers will answer to God some day for encouraging curious speculations about the return of Christ and failing to stress the necessity for "loving His appearing"!

The Bible does not approve of this modern curiosity that plays with the Scriptures and which seeks only to impress credulous and gullible audiences with the "amazing" prophetic knowledge possessed by the brother who is preaching or teaching!

I cannot think of even one lonely passage in the New Testament which speaks of Christ's revelation, manifestation, appearing, or coming that is not directly linked with moral conduct, faith, and spiritual holiness.

The appearing of the Lord Jesus on this earth once more is not an event upon which we may curiously speculate—and when we do only that we sin. The prophetic teacher who engages in speculation to excite the curiosity of his hearers without providing them with a moral application is sinning even as he preaches.

There have been enough foolish formulas advanced about the return of Christ by those who were simply curious to cause many believers to give the matter no further thought or concern. But Peter said to expect "the appearing of Jesus Christ" (1 Peter 1:7). Paul said there is a crown of righteousness laid up in glory for all those who love His appearing. John spoke of his hope of seeing Jesus and bluntly wrote: "And every man that hath this hope in him purifieth himself, even as he is pure" (1 John 3:3).

Peter linked the testing of our faith with the coming of the Lord when he wrote:

> Though now for a season, if need be, ye are in heaviness through manifold temptations: That the trial of your faith, being much more precious than of gold that perisheth, though it be tried with fire, might be found unto praise and honour and glory at the appearing of Jesus Christ.
> (1 Peter 1:6–7)

Think of the *appearing* of Christ, for here is a word which embodies an idea—an idea of such importance to Christian theology and Christian living that we dare not allow it to pass unregarded.

This word occurs frequently in the King James Version of the Bible in reference to Jesus, and has various forms—such as *appear, appeared, appearing.* The original word from which our English was translated has about seven different forms in the Greek.

CHRIST'S APPEARING AND REVELATION

But in this usage, we are concerned only with the word *appearing* in its prophetic use. Unquestionably, that is how Peter used it in this passage. Among those seven forms in the Greek there are three particular words which all told may have these meanings: "manifest; shine upon; show; become visible; a disclosure; a coming; a manifestation; a revelation."

I point this out because Peter also wrote that the Christians should "gird up the loins of [their] mind[s], be sober, and hope to the end for the grace that is to be brought unto you at the revelation of Jesus Christ" (1 Peter 1:13).

Some of you might like to ask the translators a question, but they are all dead! The question might well be, "Why was the similar form of the original word translated in one case as the *appearing* and in the other as the *revelation* of Jesus Christ?"

There may have been some very fine shade of meaning which they felt must be expressed by one word and not the other, but we may take it as truth that the words are used interchangeably in the Bible.

We do not have to belabor this point, and actually some people are in trouble in the Scriptures because they try too hard! The Lord never expected us to have to try so hard and to push on to the end of setting up a formula or a doctrinal exposition on the shades of meaning and forms of a single word.

The Bible is the easiest book in the world to understand—one of the easiest for the spiritual mind but one of the hardest for the carnal mind! I will pay no mind to those who find it necessary to strain at a shade of meaning in order to prove they are right, particularly when that position can be shown to be contrary to all the belief of Christians back to the days of the apostles.

So that is why I say it is easy to try too hard when we come to the reading and explanation of the Scriptures. So, when we come to Peter's use of this word *appearing*—just relax, for that is what it means! If a different form or word is used in another place and the same thing is being stated in a different way, it simply shows that the Holy Ghost has never been in a rut—even if interpreters are. The Spirit of God never has had to resort to clichés even though preachers often seem to specialize in them!

THE REVELATION OF JESUS CHRIST

The appearing of Jesus Christ may mean His manifestation. It may mean a shining forth, a showing, a disclosure. Yes, it may mean His coming, the revelation of Jesus Christ!

The question that must actually be answered for most people is: "Where will this appearing or coming or disclosure or revelation take place?"

Those to whom Peter wrote concerning the appearing of Christ were Christian men and women on this earth. There is no way that this can possibly be spiritualized—the scene cannot be transferred to heaven.

Peter was writing to Christians on this earth, to the saints scattered abroad by trial and persecution. He was encouraging them to endure affliction and to trust God in their sufferings, so their faith may be found of more worth than gold at the appearing of Jesus Christ.

Common sense will tell us that this appearing could only be on the earth because he was writing to people on this earth. He was not writing to angels in any heavenly sphere. He was not saying it to Gabriel but to people living on this earth.

Now, Peter also spoke of this as an event to happen in the future—that is, the future from the time in which Peter wrote nineteen centuries ago. Writing in the year AD 65, Peter placed the appearing of Christ sometime in the future after AD 65.

We are sure, then, that Peter was not referring to the appearance of Jesus at the Jordan River when John baptized Him, for that had already taken place thirty years before.

Jesus had also appeared in Jerusalem, walking among the people, talking to the Pharisees and elders, the rabbis, and the common people, but that had also taken place thirty years before. He had suddenly appeared in the temple, just when times were good, and people were coming from everywhere with money to have it exchanged in order to buy cattle or doves for sacrifice. Using only a rope, He drove the cattle and the money changers from the temple. He appeared on the Mount of Transfiguration and after His resurrection appeared to the disciples. He had made many appearances. He was there in bodily manifestation, and He did things that could be identified. He was there as a man among men. But Peter said, "He is yet to appear" for the other appearances were all thirty years in the past.

Peter was saying: "I want you to get ready in order that the trial of your faith, your afflictions, your obedience, your cross-bearing, may mean honor and glory at the appearing of Jesus Christ"—the appearing in the future!

WAITING FOR HIS RETURN

There is no reputable testimony anywhere that Jesus Christ has appeared since the events when He appeared to put away sin through the sacrifice of Himself.

Actually we haven't found anyone that says Christ appeared to him in person, except some poor fanatic who usually dies later in the mental institution. Many new cults have arisen; men have walked through the streets saying, "I am Christ." The psychiatrists have written reams and reams of case histories of men who insisted that they were Jesus Christ.

But our Lord Jesus Christ has not yet appeared the second time, for if He had, it would have been consistent with the meaning of the word as it was commonly used in the New Testament. He would have to appear as He appeared in the temple, as He appeared by the Jordan or on the Mount of Transfiguration. It would have to be as He once appeared to His disciples after the resurrection—in visible, human manifestation, having dimension so He could be identified by the human eye and ear and touch.

If the word *appearing* is going to mean what it universally means, the appearing of Jesus Christ has to be very much the same as His appearing on the earth the first time, nearly two thousand years ago.

When He came the first time, He walked among men. He took babies in His arms. He healed the sick and the afflicted and the lame. He blessed people, ate with them, and walked among them, and the Scriptures tell us that when He appears again He will appear in the same manner. He will be a man again, though a glorified man. He will be a man who can be identified, the same Jesus as He went away.

We must also speak here of the testimonies of Christian saints through the years—of Christ being known to us in spiritual life and understanding and experience.

There is a certain sense in which everyone who has a pure heart "looks upon" God. There are bound to be those who will say, "Jesus is so real to me that I have seen Him!" I know what you mean and I thank God for it—that God has illuminated the eyes of your spiritual understanding—and you have seen Him in that sense. "Blessed are the pure in heart: for they shall see God" (Matt. 5:8).

I believe that it is entirely possible for the eyes of our faith, the understanding of our spirit, to be so illuminated that we can gaze upon our Lord—perhaps veiled, perhaps not as clearly as in that day to come, but the eyes of our heart see Him!

So, Christ does appear to people in that context. He appears when we pray and we can sense His presence. But that is not what Peter meant in respect to his second appearing upon the earth. Peter's language of that event calls for a shining forth, a revelation, a sudden coming, a visible appearance! Peter meant the same kind of appearance that the newspapers noted in the appearance of the president of the United States in Chicago. He meant the same kind of appearance which the newspapers noted when the young sergeant appeared suddenly to the delight of his family after having been away for more than two years. There has not been any appearance of Jesus like that since He appeared to put away sins by the sacrifice of Himself!

This is the gist of the Bible teaching on the second coming—we may expect an appearing!

We can sum this up and say that there is to be an appearance—in person, on earth, according to Peter—to believing persons later than Peter's time. That appearing has not yet occurred and Peter's words are still valid.

We may, therefore, expect Jesus Christ again to appear on earth to living persons as He first appeared.

My brethren, I believe that this is the gist of the Bible teaching on the second coming—we may expect an appearing! In Peter's day, the Lord had not yet returned, but they were expecting Him. Peter said He would appear.

JUDGMENT FOR THE LIVING AND DEAD

When Paul wrote to Timothy in his second letter, we find some of the dearest and most gracious words of the entire Bible:

> I charge thee therefore before God, and the Lord Jesus Christ, who shall judge the quick and the dead at his appearing and his kingdom; Preach the word; be instant in season, out of season; reprove, rebuke, exhort with all long suffering and doctrine. For the time will come when they will not endure sound doctrine. (2 Tim. 4:1–3)

Here the apostle cautions that our Lord Jesus Christ will judge the living and the dead at His appearing, and then he links that appearing and judgment with the earnest exhortation that Timothy must preach the Word, being prepared in season and out of season.

A bit later, Paul writes more about events to happen when Jesus Christ appears. He wrote:

> I have fought a good fight, I have finished my course, I have kept the faith: Henceforth there is laid up for me a crown of righteousness, which the Lord, the righteous judge, shall give me at that day: and not to me only, but unto all them also that love his appearing. (2 Tim. 4:7–8)

It is plainly stated, brethren: those who love the appearing of Jesus Christ are those who shall also receive a crown.

There are some who would like to open this up: "Doesn't it really mean anyone who believes in the premillennial position will receive the crown of righteousness?"

I say no! It means that those who are found loving the appearing of Jesus will receive the crown of righteousness! It is questionable to my mind whether some who hold a premillennial position and can argue for it can be included with those whose spirit of humility and consecration and hunger for God is quietly discernible in their love and expectation of the soon coming of their Savior.

I fear that we have gone to seed on this whole matter of His return. Why is it that such a small proportion of Christian ministers ever feel the necessity to preach a sermon on the truth of His second coming? Why should pastors depend in this matter upon those who travel around the country with their colored charts and their object lessons and their curious interpretations of Bible prophecy?

Should we not dare to believe what the apostle John wrote, that "we shall be like him; for we shall see him as he is" (1 John 3:2)?

Beloved, we are the sons of God now, for our faith is in the Son of God, Jesus Christ! We believe in Him and we rest upon Him, and yet it doth not yet appear what we shall be; but we know that when He shall appear, when He shall be disclosed, we shall be like Him, for we shall see Him as He is.

Then, John says bluntly and clearly: "And every man that hath this hope in him purifieth himself, even as he is pure" (v. 3). Everybody! Every man, he says! He singularizes it. Every man that has this hope in him purifies himself as He is pure.

Those who are expecting the Lord Jesus Christ to come and who look for that coming moment by moment and who long for that coming will be busy purifying themselves. They will not be indulging in curious speculations—they will be in preparation, purifying themselves!

It may be helpful to use an illustration here.

A wedding is about to take place and the bride is getting dressed. Her mother is nervous and there are other relatives and helpers who are trying to make sure that the bride is dressed just right.

Why all this helpful interest and concern?

Well, the bride and those around her know that she is about to go out to meet her groom, and everything must be perfectly in order. She even walks cautiously so that nothing gets out of place in dress and veil. She is preparing, for she awaits in loving anticipation and expectation the meeting with this man at the altar.

Now John says, through the Holy Ghost, that he that has this hope in him purifies and prepares himself. How? Even as He is pure!

The bride wants to be dressed worthy of the bridegroom, and so it is with the groom as well! Should not the church of

Jesus Christ be dressed worthy of her bridegroom, even as He is dressed? Pure—even as He is pure?

We are assured that the appearing of Jesus Christ will take place. It will take place in His time. There are many who believe that it can take place soon—that there is not anything which must yet be done in this earth to make possible His coming.

It will be the greatest event in the history of the world, barring His first coming and the events of His death and resurrection.

We may well say that the next greatest event in the history of the world will be the appearing of Jesus Christ: "Though now ye see him not, yet believing, ye rejoice with joy unspeakable and full of glory" (1 Peter 1:8).

The world will not know it, but he that has this hope in him will know it for he has purified himself even as Christ is pure!

REATOR OF HEAVEN AND EARTH; AND IN JESUS CHR

.

IS ONLY SON, OUR LO

HO WAS CONCEIVED BY THE HOLY SPI

ORN FROM THE VIRGIN MA

UFFERED UNDER PONTIUS PIL

AS CRUCIFIED, DEAD AND BUR

ESCENDED INTO HELL, ON THE THIRD

OSE AGAIN FROM THE DE

SCENDED TO HEAV

TS AT THE RIGHT H

F GOD THE FATHER ALMIGH

HENCE HE WILL COME TO JU

HE LIVING AND THE DE

BELIEVE IN THE HOLY SPI

HE HOLY CATHOLIC CHUR

HE COMMUNION OF SAIN

HE REMISSION OF S

HE RESURRECTION OF THE FLE

7

THE COMMUNION
OF THE CHURCH

I believe in the Holy Ghost: The holy catholic church;
The communion of saints

It would be difficult if not altogether impossible for us today to know exactly what was in the minds of the church fathers who introduced these words into the creed, but in the book of Acts we have a description of the first Christian communion: "Then they that gladly received his word were baptized: and the same day there were added unto them about three thousand souls. And they continued stedfastly in the apostles' doctrine and fellowship, and in breaking of bread, and in prayers" (Acts 2:41–42).

Here is the original apostolic fellowship, the pattern after which every true Christian communion must be modeled.

The word "fellowship," in spite of its abuses, is still a beautiful and meaningful word. When rightly understood it means the same as the word "communion"—that is, the act and condition of sharing together in some common blessing by numbers of persons. The communion of saints, then, means an intimate and loving sharing together of certain spiritual blessings by persons who are on an equal footing before the blessing in which they share. This fellowship must include every member of the church of God from Pentecost to this present moment and on to the end of the age.

Now, before there can be *communion* there must be *union*. The sharers are one in a sense altogether above organization, nationality, race, or denomination. That oneness is a divine thing, achieved by the Holy Spirit in the act of regeneration. Whoever is born of God is one with everyone else who is born of God. Just as gold is always gold, wherever and in whatever shape it is found, and every detached scrap of gold belongs to the true family and is composed of the same elements, so every regenerate soul belongs to the universal Christian community and to the fellowship of the saints.

Every redeemed soul is born out of the same spiritual life as every other redeemed soul and partakes of the divine nature in exactly the same manner. Each one is thus made a member of the Christian community and a sharer in everything which that community enjoys. This is the true communion of saints. But to know this is not enough. If we would enter into the power of it we must exercise ourselves in this truth; we must *practice* thinking and praying with the thought that we are members of the body of Christ and brothers to all the ransomed saints living and dead who have believed on Christ and acknowledged Him as Lord.

We have said that the communion of saints is a fellowship, a sharing in certain divinely given things by divinely called persons. Now, what are those things?

FELLOWSHIP OF LIFE

The first and most important is *life*—"the life of God in the soul of man," to borrow a phrase from Henry Scougal. This life is the basis of everything else that is given and shared. And that life is nothing else than God Himself. It should be evident that there can be no true Christian sharing unless there is first an impartation of life. An organization and a name do not make a church. One hundred religious persons knit into a unity by careful organization do not constitute a church any more than eleven dead men make a football team. The first requisite is life, always.

FELLOWSHIP OF TRUTH

The apostolic fellowship is also a fellowship of *truth*. The inclusiveness of the fellowship must always be held along with the exclusiveness of it. Truth brings into its gracious circle all who admit and accept the Bible as the source of all truth and the Son of God as the Savior of men. But there dare be no weak compromise with the facts, no sentimental mouthing of the old phrases: "We are all headed for the same place. Each one is seeking in his own way to please the Father and make heaven his home." The truth makes men free, and the truth will bind and loose, will open and shut, will include and exclude at its high will without respect to persons. To reject or deny the truth of the Word is to exclude ourselves from the apostolic communion.

Now, someone may ask, "What is the truth of which you speak? Is my fate to depend upon Baptist truth or Presbyterian truth or Anglican truth, or all of these or none of these? To know the communion of saints must I believe in Calvinism or Armin-ianism? In the Congregational or the Episcopal form of church government? Must I interpret prophecy in accord with the premil-lenarians or the postmillenarians? Must I believe in immersion or sprinkling or pouring?" The answer to all this is easy. The confu-sion is only apparent, not actual.

The early Christians, under the fire of persecution, driven from place to place, sometimes deprived of the opportunity for careful instruction in the faith, wanted a "rule" that would sum up all that they must believe to assure their everlasting welfare. Out of this critical need arose the creeds. Of the many, the Apostles' Creed is the best known and best loved, and has been reverently repeated by the largest number of believers through the centuries. And for millions of good men, that creed contains the essentials of truth. Not all truths, to be sure, but the heart of all truth. It served in trying days as a kind of secret password that instantly united men to each other when passed from lip to lip by the followers of the Lamb. It is fair to say, then, that the truth shared by saints in the apostolic fellowship is the same truth that is outlined for convenience in the Apostles' Creed.

Of the many, the Apostles' Creed is the best known and best loved, and has been reverently repeated by the largest number of believers through the centuries.

In this day, when the truth of Christi-anity is under serious fire from so many directions, it is most important that we know what we believe and that we guard it carefully. But in our effort to interpret and expound the Holy Scriptures in accord with the ancient faith of all Christians, we should remember that a seeking soul may find salvation through the blood of Christ while yet knowing little of the fuller teachings of Christian theology. We must, therefore, admit to our fellowship every sheep who has heard the voice of the Shepherd and has tried to follow Him. The beginner in Christ who has not yet had time to learn much Christian truth, and the underprivileged believer who has had the misfortune to be brought up in a church where the Word has been neglected from the pulpit, are very much in the same situation. Their faith grasps only a small portion of truth, and their "sharing" is necessarily limited to the small portion they grasp. The important thing, however, is that the little bit they do enjoy is *real truth*. It may be no more than this, that "Christ Jesus came into the world to save sinners" (1 Tim. 1:15); but if they walk in the light of that much truth, no more is required to bring them into the circle of the blessed and to constitute them true members of the apostolic fellowship.

FELLOWSHIP OF PRESENCE

True Christian communion consists in the sharing of a *presence*. This is not poetry merely, but a fact taught in bold letters in the New Testament. God has given us Himself in the person of His Son. "Where two or three are gathered together in my name, there am I in the midst of them" (Matt. 18:20). The immanence of God in His universe makes possible the enjoyment of the "real presence" by the saints of God in heaven and on earth simultaneously. Wherever they may be, He is present to them in the fullness of His Godhead.

I do not believe that the Bible teaches the possibility of communication between the saints on earth and those in heaven.

But while there cannot be communication, there most surely can be communion. Death does not tear the individual believer from his place in the body of Christ. As in our human bodies each member is nourished by the same blood that at once gives life and unity to the entire organism, so in the body of Christ the quickening Spirit flowing through every part gives life and unity to the whole. Our Christian brethren who have gone from our sight retain still their place in the universal fellowship. The church is one, whether waking or sleeping, by a unity of life forevermore.

> *Our Christian brethren who have gone from our sight retain still their place in the universal fellowship.*

MUTUAL BELONGING

The most important thing about the doctrine of the communion of saints is its practical effects on the lives of Christians. We know very little about the saints above, but about the saints on earth we know, or can know, a great deal. We Protestants do not believe (since the Bible does not teach) that the saints who have gone into heaven before us are in any way affected by the prayers or labors of saints who remain on earth. Our particular care is not for those whom God has already honored with the vision beatific, but for the hard-pressed and struggling pilgrims who are still traveling toward the City of God. We all belong to each other; the spiritual welfare of each one is or should be the loving concern of all the rest.

We should pray for an enlargement of soul to receive into our hearts all of God's people, whatever their race, color, or church affiliation. Then we should practice thinking of ourselves as members of the blessed family of God and should strive in prayer to love and appreciate everyone who is born of the Father. I suggest also that we try to acquaint ourselves as far as possible with the good and saintly souls who lived before our times and now belong to the company of the redeemed in heaven. How sad to limit our sympathies to those of our own day, when God in His providence has made it possible for us to enjoy the rich treasures of the minds and hearts of so many holy and gifted saints of other days. To confine our reading to the works of a few favorite authors of today or last week is to restrict our horizons and to pinch our souls dangerously.

I have no doubt that the prayerful reading of some of the great spiritual classics of the centuries would destroy in us forever that constriction of soul that seems to be the earmark of modern evangelicalism.

> *To confine our reading to the works of a few favorite authors of today or last week is to restrict our horizons and to pinch our souls dangerously.*

For many of us the wells of the past wait to be reopened. Augustine, for instance, would bring to us a sense of the overwhelming majesty of God that would go far to cure the flippancy of spirit found so widely among modern Christians. Bernard of Cluny would sing to us of "Jerusalem the Golden" and the peace of an eternal sabbath day until the miserable pleasures of this world become intolerable; Richard Rolle would show us how to escape from the "abundance of riches, flattering of women, the fairness and beauty of youth," that we may go on to know God with an intimacy that will become in our hearts "heat, fragrance and song"; Tersteegen would whisper to us of the "hidden love of God" and the awful presence until our hearts would become "still before Him" and "prostrate inwardly adore Him"; before our eyes the sweet St. Francis would throw his arms of love around sun and moon, trees and rain, bird and beast, and thank God for them all in a pure rapture of spiritual devotion.

But who is able to complete the roster of the saints? To them we owe a debt of gratitude too great to comprehend: prophet and apostle, martyr and reformer, scholar and translator, hymnist and composer, teacher and evangelist, not to mention ten thousand times ten thousand simplehearted and anonymous souls who kept the flame of pure religion alive even in those times when the faith of our fathers was burning but dimly all over the world.

They belong to us, all of them, and we belong to them. They and we and all redeemed men and women of whatever age or clime are included in the universal fellowship of Christ, and together compose "a royal priesthood, an holy nation, a peculiar people" (1 Peter 2:9), who enjoy a common but blessed communion of saints.

EATOR OF HEAVEN AND EARTH; AND IN JESUS CHRI

S   ONLY   SON,   OUR   LO

O   WAS   CONCEIVED   BY   THE   HOLY   SPIR

RN   FROM   THE   VIRGIN   MA

FFERED   UNDER   PONTIUS   PILA

S   CRUCIFIED,   DEAD   AND   BURI

SCENDED   INTO   HELL,   ON   THE   THIRD

SE   AGAIN   FROM   THE   DE

CENDED   TO   HEAV

TS   AT   THE   RIGHT   H

       GOD   THE   FATHER   ALMIGH

ENCE   HE   WILL   COME   TO   JU

E   LIVING   AND   THE   DE

       BELIEVE   IN   THE   HOLY   SPI

HE   HOLY   CATHOLIC   CHUR

HE   COMMUNION   OF   SAI

HE   REMISSION   OF   S

HE   RESURRECTION   OF   THE   FL

...REATOR OF HEAVEN AND EARTH; AND IN JESUS CHR...

...S ONLY SON, OUR LO...

...HO WAS CONCEIVED BY THE HOLY SPI...

...ORN FROM THE VIRGIN MA...

...FFERED UNDER PONTIUS PILA...

...AS CRUCIFIED, DEAD AND BURI...

...SCENDED INTO HELL, ON THE THIRD...

...SE AGAIN FROM THE DE...

...CENDED TO HEAV...

...TS AT THE RIGHT HA...

...GOD THE FATHER ALMIGH...

...ENCE HE WILL COME TO JU...

...E LIVING AND THE DE...

...BELIEVE IN THE HOLY SPIR...

...E HOLY CATHOLIC CHUR...

...E COMMUNION OF SAIN...

...E REMISSION OF SI...

...E RESURRECTION OF THE FLE...

8

FORGIVENESS

The forgiveness of sins

Paul identifies Jesus Christ as the Savior "who gave himself for us, that he might redeem us from all iniquity, and purify unto himself a peculiar people, zealous of good works" (Titus 2:14).

We can quickly learn the value of any object by the price which people are willing to pay for it. You may remember the story about the rooster scratching around in the barnyard for kernels of corn. Suddenly he scratched up a beautiful pearl of fabulous price which had been lost years before, but he just pushed it aside and kept on looking for corn. The pearl had no value for the rooster, although it had a great value for those who had set a price upon it.

In the various markets in the world, something which has no value for a disinterested person may be considered of great value by the person desiring it and purchasing it. It is in this sense, then, that we learn how dear and precious we are to Christ by what He was willing to give for us.

I believe many Christians are tempted to downgrade themselves too much. I am not arguing against true humility, and my word to you is this: think as little of yourself as you want to, but always remember that our Lord Jesus Christ thought very highly of you—enough to give Himself for you in death and sacrifice.

If the devil does come to you and whispers that you are no good, don't argue with him. In fact, you may as well admit it, but then remind the devil: "Regardless of what you say about me, I must tell you how the Lord feels about me. He tells me that I am so valuable to Him that He gave Himself for me on the cross!"

So the value is set by the price paid—and, in our case, the price paid was our Lord Himself! The end that the Savior had in view was that He would redeem us from all iniquity—that is, from the power and consequences of iniquity.

FORGIVENESS AND THE DOUBLE CURE

We often sing the words "Rock of Ages" by Augustus M. Toplady, in which the death of our Lord Jesus is described as "the double cure" for sin. I think many people sing the hymn without realizing what Toplady meant by the double cure.

> Be of sin the double cure
> Save from wrath and make me pure.

The wrath of God against sin and then the power of sin in the human life—these both must be cured. Therefore, when He gave Himself for us, He redeemed us with a double cure, delivering us from the consequences of sin and delivering us from the power which sin exercises in human lives.

Now, Paul, in this great nugget of spiritual truth, reminds us that the redemptive Christ performs a purifying work in the people of God. You will have to agree with me that one of the deep and outbroken diseases of this present world and society is impurity, and it displays itself in dozens of symptoms. We are prone to look upon certain lewd and indecent physical actions as the impurities which plague human life and society—but the actual lusting and scheming and planning and plotting come from a far deeper source of impurity within the very minds and innermost beings of sinful men and women. If we were people of clean hands and pure hearts, we would be intent upon doing the things that please God. Impurity is not just a wrong action; impurity is the state of mind and heart and soul which is just the opposite of purity and wholeness.

He would redeem us from all iniquity— that is, from the power and consequences of iniquity.

Sexual misconduct is a symptom of the disease of impurity—but so is hatred. Pride and egotism, resentfulness and churlishness come to the surface out of sinful and impure minds and hearts, just as gluttony and slothfulness and self-indulgence do. All of these and countless others come to the surface as outward symptoms of the deep, inward disease of selfishness and sin.

Because this is a fact in life and experience, it is the spiritual work of Jesus Christ to purify His people by His own blood to rid them of this deep-lying disease. That is why He is called the Great Physician—He is able to heal us of this plague of impurity and iniquity, redeeming us from the consequences of our sins and purifying us from the presence of our sins.

Now, brethren, either this is true and realizable in human life and experience, or Christianity is the cheap fraud of the day. Either it is true and a dependable spiritual option, or we should fold up the Bible and put it away with other classical pieces of literature which have no particular validity in the face of death.

Thank God that there are millions who dare to stand as if in a great chorus and shout with me, "It is true! He did give Himself to redeem us from all iniquity and He does perform this purifying work in our lives day by day!"

FORGIVENESS WITHOUT REGRET

The human heart is heretical by nature. Popular religious beliefs should be checked carefully against the Word of God, for they are almost certain to be wrong.

Legalism, for instance, is natural to the human heart. Grace, in its true New Testament meaning, is foreign to human reason, not because it is contrary to reason but because it lies beyond it. The doctrine of grace had to be revealed; it could not have been discovered.

When moral innocence has been restored by the forgiving love of God the guilt may be remembered, but the sting is gone from the memory.

The essence of legalism is self-atonement. The seeker tries to make himself acceptable to God by some act of restitution, or by self-punishment, or the feeling of regret. The desire to be pleasing to God is commendable, certainly, but the effort to please God by self-effort is not, for it assumes that sin once done may be undone, an assumption wholly false.

Long after we have learned from the Scriptures that we cannot by fasting, or the wearing of the hair short, or the making of many prayers, atone for the sins of the soul, we still tend by a kind of pernicious natural heresy to feel that we can please God and purify our souls by the penance of perpetual regret.

This latter is the Protestant's unacknowledged penance. Though he claims to believe in the doctrine of justification by faith he still secretly feels that what he calls "godly sorrow" will make him dear to God. Though he may know better, he is caught in the web of a wrong religious feeling and betrayed.

There is indeed a godly sorrow that worketh repentance (2 Cor. 7:10), and it must be acknowledged that among us Christians this feeling is often not present in sufficient strength to work real repentance; but the persistence of this sorrow till it becomes chronic regret is neither right nor good. Regret is a kind of frustrated repentance that has not been quite consummated. Once the soul has turned from all sin and committed itself wholly to God, there is no longer any legitimate place for regret. When moral innocence has been restored by the forgiving love of God the guilt may be remembered, but the sting is gone from the memory. The forgiven man knows that he has sinned, but he no longer feels it.

The effort to be forgiven by works is one that can never be completed, because no one knows or can know how much is enough to cancel out the offense; so the seeker must go on year after year paying on his moral debt, here a little, there a little, knowing that he sometimes adds to his bill much more than he pays. The task of keeping books on such a transaction can never end, and the seeker can only hope that when the last entry is made he may be ahead and the account fully paid. This is quite the popular belief, this forgiveness by self-effort, but it is a natural heresy and can at last only betray those who depend upon it.

It may be argued that the absence of regret indicates a low and inadequate view of sin, but the exact opposite is true. Sin is so frightful, so destructive to the soul, that no human thought or act can in any degree diminish its lethal effects. Only God can deal with it successfully; only the blood of Christ can cleanse it from the pores of the spirit. The heart that has been delivered from this dread enemy feels not regret but wondrous relief and unceasing gratitude.

The returned prodigal honors his father more by rejoicing than by repining. Had the young man in the story had less faith in his father he might have mourned in a corner instead of joining in the festivities. His confidence in the loving-kindness of his father gave him the courage to forget his checkered past.

Regret frets the soul as tension frets the nerves and anxiety the mind. I believe that the chronic unhappiness of most Christians may be attributed to a gnawing uneasiness lest God has not fully forgiven them, or the fear that He expects as the price of His forgiveness some sort of emotional penance which they have not furnished. As our confidence in the goodness of God mounts, our anxieties will diminish, and our moral happiness rise in inverse proportion.

Regret may be no more than a form of self-love. A man may have such a high regard for himself that any failure to live up to his own image of himself disappoints him deeply. He feels that he has betrayed his better self by his act of wrongdoing, and even if God is willing to forgive him, he will not forgive himself. Sin brings to such a man a painful loss of face that is not soon forgotten. He becomes permanently angry with himself and tries to punish himself by going to God frequently with petulant self-accusations. This state of mind crystallizes finally into a feeling of chronic regret which appears to be a proof of deep penitence but is actually proof of deep self-love.

Regret for a sinful past will remain until we truly believe that for us in Christ that sinful past no longer exists. The man in Christ has only Christ's past, and that is perfect and acceptable to God. In Christ he died. In Christ he rose, and in Christ he is seated within the circle of God's favored ones. He is no longer angry with himself because he is no longer self-regarding, but Christ-regarding; hence there is no place for regret.

FORGIVENESS AND OUR FUTURE HOPE

Christians ought to know and understand God's reasoning and philosophy behind His eternal provision for His children. I am not happy with the attitude of some Christians who are little more than parrots concerning the truths of God.

Some people think it is spiritual just to accept all of the dogmas without any real thought or comprehension—"Yes, I believe it. The Bible says it and I believe it."

We are supposed to be mature and growing Christians, able to give an answer with comprehension concerning our faith. We are supposed to be more than parrots.

The parrot in the pet shop can be taught to quote John 3:16 or portions of the Apostles' Creed if you give him tidbits as a reward. If all we want is to have someone feed truth into us without knowing or understanding why it is like it is, then we are simply Christian parrots saying "I believe! I believe!"

I think we Christians should spend a lot more time thinking about the meaning and implications of our faith, and if we ask God Almighty to help us, we will know why He has dealt with us as He has and why the future holds bright promise for God's children.

We are redeemed by the blood of the Lamb, our yesterdays behind us, our sin under the blood forever and a day, to be remembered against us no more forever.

God sent His Son to redeem us and to make us whole again. Some people seem to think that Jesus came only to reclaim us or restore us so that we could regain the original image of Adam. Let me remind you that Jesus Christ did infinitely more in His death and resurrection than just undoing the damage of the fall. He came to raise us into the image of Jesus Christ, not merely to the image of the first Adam. The first man Adam was a living soul, the second man Adam was a life-giving Spirit. The first man Adam was made of the earth, but the second man is the Lord from heaven!

Redemption in Christ, then, is not to pay back dollar for dollar, or to straighten man out and restore him into Adamic grace. The purpose and work of redemption in Christ Jesus is to raise man as much above the level of Adam as Christ Himself is above the level of Adam. We are to gaze upon Christ, not Adam, and in so doing are being transformed by the Spirit of God into Christ's image.

So, we can say that earth may have been good enough for that creature who was created from the dust and clay, but it is not good enough for the living soul who is redeemed by royal blood! Earth was fit and proper to be the eternal dwelling place for that creature who was made by God's hand, but it is not appropriate nor sufficient to be the eternal dwelling place of that redeemed being who is begotten of the Holy Ghost. Every born-again Christian has been lifted up—lifted up from the level of the fallen Adamic race to the heavenly plane of the unfallen and victorious Christ. He belongs up there!

But, in the meantime, sin separates body and soul. That is why the Lord Jesus Christ, as He was about to leave the earth after His resurrection, told His disciples: "In my Father's house are many mansions . . . I go to prepare a place for you. And if I go and prepare a place for you, I will come again, and receive you unto myself; that where I am, there ye may be also" (John 14:2–3).

It is an amazing thing that Jesus Christ claimed that He never left the bosom of the Father. He said the Son of Man, who is in the bosom of the Father, hath declared it. While Jesus was upon earth, walking as a man among men, by the mystery of the ever-present God and the indivisible substance of the Deity, He could remain in the bosom of the Father, and He did.

So, you and I are to be elevated and promoted. Let us not forget that it was the Lord God Almighty who made man and blew into him the breath of life so that he became a living soul. That was man—and then in redemption God raised him infinitely above that level, so that now we hear the Lord and Savior promising, "I have gone to prepare a place for you." In the time of our departure, the body that He gave us will disintegrate and drop away like a cocoon, for the spirit of the man soars away to the presence of God. The body must await that great day of resurrection at the last trump, for Paul says, "The dead shall be raised incorruptible, and we shall be changed" (1 Cor. 15:52).

With the promises of God so distinct and beautiful, it is unbecoming that a Christian should make such a fearful thing of death. The fact that we Christians do display a neurosis about dying indicates that we are not where we ought to be spiritually. If we had actually reached a place of such spiritual commitment that the wonders of heaven were so close that we longed for the illuminating presence of our Lord, we would not go into such a fearful and frantic performance every time we find something wrong with our physical frame.

I do not think that a genuine, committed Christian ever ought to be afraid to die. We do not have to be, because Jesus promised that He would prepare a proper place for all of those who shall be born again, raised up out of the agony and stress of this world through the blood of the everlasting covenant into that bright and gracious world above.

Notice that Jesus said, "In my Father's house are many mansions." If it is His Father's house, it is also our Father's house because the Lord Jesus is our elder brother. Jesus also said, "I go to my Father and your Father—my God and your God" (see John 20:17). If the Father's house is the house of Jesus, it is also the house of all of His other sons and daughters.

Yes, we Christians are much better off than we really know—and there are a great many things here below that we can get along without and not be too shaken about it if we are honestly committed to the promises concerning the Father's house and its many dwelling places. It is one of the sad commentaries on our times that Christians can actually be foolish enough to get their affections so centered upon the things of this earth that they forget how quickly their time in this body and upon this earth will flee away.

I am sure that our Lord is looking for heavenly minded Christians. His Word encourages us to trust Him with such a singleness of purpose that He is able to deliver us from the fear of death and the uncertainties of tomorrow. I believe He is up there preparing me a mansion—

He is fitting up my mansion,
Which eternally shall stand,
For my stay shall not be transient
In that holy, happy land.

Read again what John said about his vision of the future to come.

I saw a new heaven and a new earth: for the first heaven and the first earth were passed away; and there was no more sea. And I John saw the holy city, the new Jerusalem, coming down from God out of heaven, prepared as a bride adorned for her husband. (Rev. 21:1–2)

Brethren, I say that it is just too bad that we have relegated this passage to be read mostly at funeral services. The man who was reporting this was not on his way to a funeral—he was on his way to the New Jerusalem!

He continued: "And I heard a great voice out of heaven saying, Behold, the tabernacle of God is with men, and he will dwell with them, and they shall be his people, and God himself shall be with them, and be their God. And God shall wipe away all tears from their eyes; and there shall be no more death, neither sorrow, nor crying, neither shall there be any more pain: for the former things are passed away" (vv. 3–4).

John then describes that great and beautiful city having the glory of God, with her light like unto a stone that was most precious, even like as jasper, clear as crystal. "And I saw no temple therein: for the Lord God Almighty and the Lamb are the temple of it. And the city had no need of the sun, neither of the moon, to shine in it: for the glory of God did lighten it, and the Lamb is the light thereof" (vv. 22–23).

Ah, the people of God ought to be the happiest people in all the wide world! People should be coming to us constantly and asking the source of our joy and delight—redeemed by the blood of the Lamb, our yesterdays behind us, our sin under the blood forever and a day, to be remembered against us no more forever. God is our Father, Christ is our Brother, the Holy Ghost our Advocate and Comforter. Our Brother has gone to the Father's house to prepare a place for us, leaving with us the promise that He will come again!

Don't send Moses, Lord, don't send Moses! He broke the tables of stone.

Don't send Elijah for me, Lord! I am afraid of Elijah—he called down fire from heaven.

Don't send Paul, Lord! He is so learned that I feel like a little boy when I read his epistles.

O Lord Jesus, come yourself! I am not afraid of Thee. You took the little children as lambs to your fold. You forgave the woman taken in adultery. You healed the timid woman who reached out in the crowd to touch You. We are not afraid of You!

Even so, come, Lord Jesus! Come quickly!

REATOR OF HEAVEN AND EARTH; AND IN JESUS CHR

IS   ONLY   SON,   OUR   LO

HO   WAS   CONCEIVED   BY   THE   HOLY   SPI

ORN   FROM   THE   VIRGIN   MA

UFFERED   UNDER   PONTIUS   PILA

AS   CRUCIFIED,   DEAD   AND   BURI

ESCENDED   INTO   HELL,   ON   THE   THIRD

OSE   AGAIN   FROM   THE   DE

CENDED   TO   HEAV

TS   AT   THE   RIGHT   H

          GOD   THE   FATHER   ALMIGH

ENCE   HE   WILL   COME   TO   JU

E   LIVING   AND   THE   DE

          BELIEVE   IN   THE   HOLY   SPI

E   HOLY   CATHOLIC   CHUR

E   COMMUNION   OF   SAIN

E   REMISSION   OF   SI

E   RESURRECTION   OF   THE   FLE

9

ETERNITY

The resurrection of the body:
And the life everlasting. Amen.

When considering the resurrection of Christ and the promised future resurrection of the redeemed, we may at times
be disturbed by a sense of unreality about the whole thing. We
just cannot picture it. The thought of it is so completely unlike
anything that has occurred in our experience that our minds
cannot find a definite place to light, so they flutter over the idea
like a bird over unfamiliar terrain.

No doubt this bothers many of God's people not a little. They
fear that the mental uncertainty they feel is a proof of unbelief
and wonder whether they actually believe in the resurrection
of the body as taught in the New Testament and repeated in the
Apostles' Creed. I believe these fears are groundless. Here's why:

These "fearful saints" are confusing two things which are
wholly unlike each other, that is, they are confusing faith and

imagination. Faith is confidence in the character of a moral being, which takes the word of that being as completely trustworthy and rests in it without question. Imagination is the power to visualize, to create in the mind a picture of things unseen. We may have either one without the other. The two are not identical and are indeed only distantly related.

A soldier has been overseas two or three years and is now on his way home. As he gets closer to his native shores, anticipation mounts in his heart. He visualizes the joyous meeting soon to take place. He pictures his mother, his sister, his wife, and he smiles as he thinks of how much his little son may have grown since he saw him last. The whole scene is before him as he dreams of the long-awaited reunion. Intelligence dictates a slight difference in the appearance of his loved ones. He knows they will have changed, and he tries to adjust his mental image accordingly. He thus visualizes an event which has not yet occurred by drawing on past experience.

It is right here that thought breaks down when it comes to the resurrection. We have no experience to guide us. When Christ rose from the dead He did what no one had ever done before. We cannot imagine how He accomplished the miracle. We are not even sure exactly what wonderful thing happened there in the silence of Joseph's new tomb. That He came forth, alive forevermore, has been the firmly settled faith of the church from the beginning. How He accomplished it is a secret locked in the mind of God. We should remember the wise admonition of John Wesley: "Let us not doubt a fact because we do not know how it was accomplished." The resurrection of Christ is a fact. More than that we need not know.

Our own future resurrection is even harder to visualize. To paint a mental picture of our death is not so difficult because it has been our experience that everyone goes out that way.

Thou know'st 'tis common—all that lives must die,
Passing through nature to eternity.

The mind can visualize our departure from this earth because it has something to guide it in forming its mental picture, but the resurrection affords it no familiar stuff with which to work. And here is where anxiety and self-reproach enter. Because we cannot visualize it, we are afraid that we do not believe it.

The hope of the resurrection is a matter of pure faith. It rests upon the character of God and draws its comfort from the knowledge that God cannot lie nor deceive nor change. He has promised that all who sleep in Jesus shall be brought again from their graves to meet the Lord in the air and be with Him forever. The New Testament is filled with this joyful expectation. How God will bring it all to pass is not for us to know. We are not called to understand, but to believe.

Though a detailed knowledge of the mysterious ways of God in accomplishing the resurrection were possible for us, I wonder if we would be any better off for it. We honor God more by believing Him to do the impossible. And after all, nothing is impossible with God.

OUR FUTURE HOPE

God being a God of infinite goodness must, by the necessity of His nature, will for each of His creatures the fullest measure of happiness consistent with its capacities and with the happiness of all other creatures.

Furthermore, being omniscient and omnipotent, God has the wisdom and power to achieve whatever He wills. The redemption that He wrought for us through the incarnation, death, and resurrection of His only begotten Son guarantees eternal blessedness to all who through faith become beneficiaries of that redemption.

This the church teaches her children to believe, and her teaching is more than hopeful thinking. It is founded upon the fullest and plainest revelations of the Old and New Testaments. That it accords with the most sacred yearnings of the human heart does not in any manner weaken it, but serves rather to confirm the truth of it, since the One who made the heart might be expected also to make provision for the fulfillment of its deepest longings.

While Christians believe this in a general way, it is still difficult for them to visualize life as it will be in heaven, and it is especially hard for them to picture themselves as inheriting such bliss as the Scriptures describe. The reason for this is not hard to discover. The godliest Christian is the one who knows himself best, and no one who knows himself will believe that he deserves anything better than hell.

The man who knows himself least is likely to have cheerful if groundless confidence in his own moral worth. Such a man has less trouble believing that he will inherit an eternity of bliss because his concepts are only quasi-Christian, being influenced strongly by chimney-corner Scripture and old wives' tales. He thinks of heaven as being very much like California without the heat and the smog, and himself as inhabiting a splendiferous palace with all modern conveniences, and wearing a heavily bejeweled crown. Throw in a few angels and you have the vulgar picture of the future life held by the devotees of popular Christianity.

This is the heaven that appears in the saccharine ballads of the guitar-twanging rockabilly gospellers that clutter up the religious scene today. That the whole thing is completely unrealistic and contrary to the laws of the moral universe seems to make no difference to anyone. As a pastor I have laid to rest the mortal remains of many a man whose future could not but be mighty uncertain, but who before the funeral was over nevertheless managed to get title to a mansion just over the hilltop. I have steadfastly refused to utter any word that would add to the deception, but the emotional wattage of the singing was so high that the mourners went away vaguely believing that in spite of all they knew about the deceased, everything would be all right some bright morning.

No one who has felt the weight of his own sin or heard from Calvary the Savior's mournful cry, "My God, my God, why hast thou forsaken me?" (Mark 15:34), can ever allow his soul to rest on the feeble hope popular religion affords. He will—indeed he must—insist upon forgiveness and cleansing and the protection the vicarious death of Christ provides.

"[God] hath made him to be sin for us, who knew no sin; that we might be made the righteousness of God in him" (2 Cor. 5:21). So wrote Paul, and Luther's great outburst of faith shows what this can mean in a human soul. "O Lord," cried Luther, "Thou art my righteousness, I am Thy sin."

Any valid hope of a state of blessedness beyond the incident of death must lie in the goodness of God and the work of atonement accomplished for us by Jesus Christ on the cross. The deep, deep love of God is the fountain out of which flows our future beatitude, and the grace of God in Christ is the channel by which it reaches us. The cross of Christ creates a moral situation where every attribute of God is on the side of the returning sinner. Even justice is on our side, for it is written, "If we confess our sins, he is faithful and just to forgive us our sins, and to cleanse us from all unrighteousness" (1 John 1:9).

The true Christian may safely look forward to a future state that is as happy as perfect love wills it to be. Since love cannot desire for its object anything less than the fullest possible measure of enjoyment for the longest possible time, it is virtually beyond our power to conceive of a future as consistently delightful as that which Christ is preparing for us. And who is to say what is possible with God?

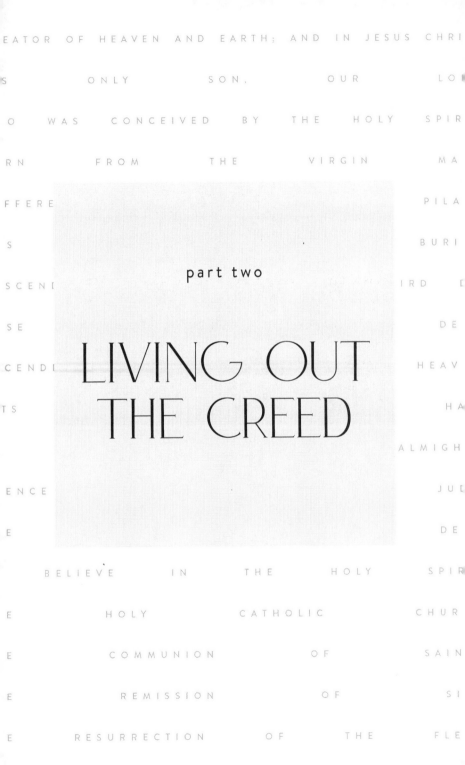

EATOR OF HEAVEN AND EARTH; AND IN JESUS CHRI

S   ONLY   SON,   OUR   LO

O   WAS   CONCEIVED   BY   THE   HOLY   SPIR

RN   FROM   THE   VIRGIN   MA

FFERE   PILA

S   BURI

SCENI   IRD   [

SE   DE

CENDI   HEAV

TS   HA

                                                    ALMIGH

ENCE   JU[

E   DE

BELIEVE   IN   THE   HOLY   SPIR

E   HOLY   CATHOLIC   CHUR

E   COMMUNION   OF   SAIN

E   REMISSION   OF   SI

E   RESURRECTION   OF   THE   FLE

part two

LIVING OUT
THE CREED

REATOR OF HEAVEN AND EARTH; AND IN JESUS CHR

IS ONLY SON, OUR LO

HO WAS CONCEIVED BY THE HOLY SPI

ORN FROM THE VIRGIN MA

UFFERED UNDER PONTIUS PILA

AS CRUCIFIED, DEAD AND BUR

ESCENDED INTO HELL, ON THE THIRD

OSE AGAIN FROM THE DE

SCENDED TO HEAV

TS AT THE RIGHT H

F GOD THE FATHER ALMIGH

HENCE HE WILL COME TO JU

E LIVING AND THE DE

BELIEVE IN THE HOLY SPI

E HOLY CATHOLIC CHUR

E COMMUNION OF SAIN

E REMISSION OF SI

E RESURRECTION OF THE FLE

10

LET'S BE HUMBLE ABOUT OUR ORTHODOXY

Christianity is rarely found pure apart from Christ and His inspired apostles; probably no believer or company of believers in the history of the world has ever held the truth in total purity.

One great saint believed that the truth is so vast and mighty that no one is capable of taking it all in, and that it requires the whole company of ransomed souls properly to reflect the whole body of revealed truth.

The light has shone upon men and nations, and (God be praised) it has shone with sufficient clarity to enable millions to travel home in its glow; but no believer, however pure his heart or however obedient his life, has ever been able to receive it as it shines from the throne unmodified by his own mental stuff. As a lump of clay when grasped by the human hand remains clay but cannot escape the imprint of the hand, so the truth of God when grasped by the human mind remains truth but bears upon it the image of the mind that grasps it. Truth cannot enter a passive mind. It must be received into the mind by an active mental response, and the act of receiving it tends to alter it to a greater or lesser degree. As the sun's rays are bent when passing through a prism, so has the light of God been bent when passing through the hearts of men. Sin, temperament, prejudice, early education, cultural influences, prevailing vogues—all have worked to throw the eyes of the heart out of focus and distort the inward vision.

Of course, I refer here to theological and religious truth. How pure this truth is in any place at any given time is revealed by the moral standards of those who hold the truth and by religious practices among the churches generally. Spiritual truth (by which I mean the disclosures of the Holy Spirit to the human spirit) is always the same. The Spirit always says the same thing to whomsoever He speaks and altogether without regard to passing doctrinal emphases or theological vogues. He flashes the beauty of Christ upon the wondering heart, and the awed spirit receives it with a minimum of interference. Wesley and Watts were worlds apart in their theology, but they could and did love and sing the same hymns of pure worship and adoration. The Spirit united them to worship even though their respective views of truth separated them doctrinally.

The Spirit always says the same thing to whomsoever He speaks. . . . The Holy Spirit is the true conservator of orthodoxy.

Each age has interpreted Christianity after its own fashion. The religion of the barnstorming American revivalists of the nineteenth century was certainly something different from that of Luther or the medieval mystics or the apostolic fathers. The bishops who met at Nicea in the fourth century to defend the faith of Christ from the attack of the Arians surely differed radically from the scholars and saints who stood to defend that same faith from the attack of the higher critics in the early twentieth century.

Theology has a tendency to run to modes just as does philosophy. The Christian teachers of the Middle Ages bore down hard upon the vanity of life and the innate wickedness of the body. In the early days of America, the prevailing doctrine was hell, and the popular preachers of those times revealed more details about that terrible place than were known to the inspired writers of the Scriptures. In more recent times, it was discovered again that God is love, and the love of God for mankind became the chief theme of sermons and song throughout the evangelical world.

Right now we are in another period of transition, and blessed is the man that knows where we are going. Whatever direction the theological wind may set, there are two things of which we may be certain: One is that God will not leave Himself without a witness. There will always be some who hold the creed of Christ, the inspired outline of Christian doctrine. Saving truth will never be completely hidden from the sight of men. The poor in spirit, the penitent, will always find Christ close at hand ready to save them. The other is that the Holy Spirit is the true conservator of orthodoxy and will invariably say the same thing to meek and trusting souls.

Illuminated hearts are sure to agree at the point where the light falls. Our only real danger is that we may grieve the blessed

Spirit into silence and so be left to the mercy of our intellects. Then we shall have Christian scholars in abundance, but we'll be short on adoring saints. We'll have defenders of the faith who can overawe their opponents with their logic and their learning, but we'll be without prophets and mystics and hymnists. We'll have the bush, pruned and trimmed and properly cultivated, but in the bush there will be no fire.

Truth is forever the same, but modes and emphases and interpretations vary. It is a cheering thought that Christ can adapt Himself to any race or age or people. He will give life and light to any man or woman anywhere in the world regardless of doctrinal emphasis or prevailing religious customs, provided that man or woman takes Him as He is and trusts Him without reservation. The Spirit never bears witness to an argument about Christ, but He never fails to witness to a proclamation of Christ crucified, dead, and buried, and now ascended to the right hand of the Majesty on high.

The conclusion of the matter is that we should not assume that we have all the truth and that we are mistaken in nothing. Rather we should kneel in adoration before the pierced feet of Him who is the Truth and honor Him by humble obedience to His words.

EATOR OF HEAVEN AND EARTH; AND IN JESUS CHR

S   ONLY   SON,   OUR   LO

HO   WAS   CONCEIVED   BY   THE   HOLY   SPIR

ORN   FROM   THE   VIRGIN   MA

FFERED   UNDER   PONTIUS   PILA

S   CRUCIFIED,   DEAD   AND   BURI

ESCENDED   INTO   HELL,   ON   THE   THIRD

OSE   AGAIN   FROM   THE   DE

CENDED   TO   HEAV

TS   AT   THE   RIGHT   H

F   GOD   THE   FATHER   ALMIGH

HENCE   HE   WILL   COME   TO   JU

HE   LIVING   AND   THE   DE

BELIEVE   IN   THE   HOLY   SPI

HE   HOLY   CATHOLIC   CHUR

HE   COMMUNION   OF   SAI

HE   REMISSION   OF   S

HE   RESURRECTION   OF   THE   FL

REATOR OF HEAVEN AND EARTH; AND IN JESUS CHR

S   ONLY   SON,   OUR   LO

HO   WAS   CONCEIVED   BY   THE   HOLY   SPI

RN   FROM   THE   VIRGIN   MA

FFERED   UNDER   PONTIUS   PILA

S   CRUCIFIED,   DEAD   AND   BURI

SCENDED   INTO   HELL,   ON   THE   THIRD

SE   AGAIN   FROM   THE   DE

CENDED   TO   HEAV

TS   AT   THE   RIGHT   HA

GOD   THE   FATHER   ALMIGH

ENCE   HE   WILL   COME   TO   JUD

E   LIVING   AND   THE   DE

BELIEVE   IN   THE   HOLY   SPIR

E   HOLY   CATHOLIC   CHURC

E   COMMUNION   OF   SAIN

E   REMISSION   OF   SI

E   RESURRECTION   OF   THE   FLES

11

CONNECTING OUR CREEDS TO OUR DEEDS

A man's creed is the most important thing about him. What a man *does* today may not be as important as what he *believes* today, for isolated deeds may be undone, forgiven, or otherwise atoned for; but belief determines the whole drift of our lives and so decides our destiny in the end.

There are some who boast that they have no creed, but this is equivalent to saying that they have no faith, for our creed is simply the sum total of our beliefs about life. The human mind is so constituted that it must make itself up. The religious skeptic is one who has not made up his mind about such matters as the existence of God, immortality, and human responsibility. However, the most inveterate skeptic has made up his mind on some things, and every point on which he has made up his mind is a tenet of his creed. It would probably kill the skeptic to be told that he has a creed, but he has one nonetheless, and that creed will shape his destiny at last.

Every man must have a philosophy of life, and every man does have one whether he knows it or not. That philosophy is his mental outlook, his spiritual perspective, his scale of moral values. Christianity is not only a spiritual dynamic operating to transform the life of the penitent sinner, it is also a spiritual philosophy, the loftiest and purest the mind can entertain.

We move in the direction of our inner beliefs by an inviolable law of the soul. The will does not consent to a course of conduct that violates our true creed. The heart must follow its creed, and that creed will make or break the man at last. It is impossible to secure a permanent alteration in our course of conduct until there has been a corresponding alteration in our belief about that conduct. Where the heart is caught in the grip of an evil desire, the mind will be at work changing its creed to accommodate the deed. This is a kind of moral backfiring, and it is one of the deadliest things in the world. Let a man—through weakness—sin in violation of his heart creed, and there is yet hope for him; but let him change his creed to justify his conduct, and his doom is sealed. The one is sin, and may be forgiven; the other, if persisted in, results in moral atheism from which there is no recovery.

All repentance is, at bottom, a change of creed. Repentance has been defined as a change of mind about God, Christ, self, and sin. With that change comes a reversal of our course of conduct and the acquiring of a new set of habits. When the serpent set out to achieve the fall of man, he began by changing Eve's mind on three vital points. Originally she had believed that God was good, the forbidden tree a dangerous one of which to eat, and the command of proscription a just and proper one.

When the serpent finished with her, she believed that God was unkind, the command to abstain an evidence of divine injustice, and the tree itself a tree "to be desired!" Then, and not till then, "she took of the tree and did eat." The creed decided the deed as usual.

Some good people in their zeal for the doctrine of grace have denied the place of conduct in the total scheme of redemption. "We are saved by grace alone," they say, "and our conduct cannot possibly have any effect upon our relation to God. What we believe saves us, and our deeds are not important." This kind of teaching reveals a lack of familiarity with the most elementary facts of psychology as well as a pretty bad case of blindness to the plain teachings of the Bible.

Paul called the gospel "the truth which is after godliness" (Titus 1:1). Here is the formula stated in correct order. The truth creating a code, and the code eventuating in conduct. Again it is said that after the Word had come unto the Thessalonians "in power ... and in much assurance" they "turned to God from idols to serve the living and true God" (1 Thess. 1:5, 9). The point is that the doctrine they believed controlled their subsequent conduct. And this works for evil as well as for good, depending upon whether the belief is true or false. Paul wrote of certain evil teaching that would "increase unto more ungodliness" (2 Tim. 2:15, 16).

The doctrine they believed controlled their subsequent conduct.

It is for this reason that the Bible is so rigid in its insistence upon correct doctrine. In the early church, false doctrine was considered to be one of the greatest of evils, and the false teacher was never spared. Some who presented the doctrines of grace as to leave room for an evil course of living were condemned out of hand by the apostles. Those who taught that the resurrection was already past were declared blasphemers and punished promptly and severely (1 Tim. 1:20; 2 Tim. 2:17–18).

It should be stated here that there is often a great gulf separating the nominal creed and the real creed. There are thousands of professed Christians who are affected not at all by the doctrines to which they subscribed when they entered the church. Their professed creed is not their heart creed. They are living according to an inner creed to which they have never given utterance, but which controls them as surely as the helmsman controls the ship.

The average man's creed embodies a great many things that seem to him important but which do not really matter. It is hard to decide just what does and what does not matter, but there are at least some disputed doctrinal points which the honest Bible lover will recognize as unimportant. Coats, dresses, hats, and ties, for instance, have received in some circles attention far in excess of their importance. It hardly takes the wisdom of a Solomon to see that these things are mere haberdashery and cannot possibly make the individual any better or any worse for the wearing.

The things that matter are those things that "pertain unto life and godliness," and the Bible is an authentic source book for information on all such subjects. It is clear and detailed on everything that matters; the things that do not matter are passed over by the divine Author and left to the occasion and the personal choice of the individual.

We should refuse to allow ourselves to become involved in disputes over doctrinal trifles "which minister questions, rather than godly edifying" (1 Tim. 1:4), but we must as certainly set ourselves to protect the purity of that "faith which was once delivered unto the saints" (Jude 3).

> *Faith of our fathers, we will love*
> *Both friend and foe in all our strife,*
> *And preach thee, too, as love knows how,*
> *By kindly words and virtuous life.*

The ideal for us all is to bring our beliefs into line with revealed truth as found in the sacred Scriptures, and then to bring our actions into accord with our beliefs. And God has not left us to our own devices in discovering the truth nor to our own strength in following it. He has given us the Holy Spirit to be both Guide and Helper. He will show us what to believe; and then, as we surrender to Him, He will enable us to walk in the light of it. Then will both the creed and the deed be pleasing to God.

REATOR OF HEAVEN AND EARTH; AND IN JESUS CHR

S   ONLY   SON,   OUR   LO

HO   WAS   CONCEIVED   BY   THE   HOLY   SPIR

ORN   FROM   THE   VIRGIN   MA

FFERED   UNDER   PONTIUS   PILA

AS   CRUCIFIED,   DEAD   AND   BURI

SCENDED   INTO   HELL,   ON   THE   THIRD

SE   AGAIN   FROM   THE   DE

CENDED   TO   HEAV

TS   AT   THE   RIGHT   HA

GOD   THE   FATHER   ALMIGH

ENCE   HE   WILL   COME   TO   JUD

E   LIVING   AND   THE   DE

BELIEVE   IN   THE   HOLY   SPIR

E   HOLY   CATHOLIC   CHURC

E   COMMUNION   OF   SAIN

E   REMISSION   OF   SI

E   RESURRECTION   OF   THE   FLES

DOCTRINE AT WORK AND GOING PLACES

One serious flaw in present evangelicalism is that there is an excess of ideas over acts. We are hindered by a multiplicity of words over deeds. We tend to substitute religious thinking for moral action.

The book of Joshua is a corrective to this state of inertia on the part of the church, and by our reading and meditating upon it, it may be that some of the spirit of action that fired the man Joshua may get into us.

There is very little doctrine in the book of Joshua; it is not a book of doctrine at all, per se. And yet, the book of Joshua *is* a book of doctrine. But it is doctrine in uniform. It is doctrine with a sword and a hammer. It is doctrine going somewhere and doing something.

In Joshua we see ideas in gear with reality. We see spiritual thoughts in working clothes, doing something. And if the church of the Lord Jesus Christ were to rouse itself, rub the sleep out of its eyes, put on its working clothes and get busy translating its nice religious thoughts into fine moral conduct, I believe we would have the revival we have been praying for.

Now, in Christendom we have a wonder-filled museum of theological beliefs. Once in a while, I comfort my heart by kneeling down in my study and just meditating upon the things that I believe—the things that are truly and indeed mine from the Book of God. Not my own ideas, but biblical ideas which I hold.

The sweet, heavenly thoughts about God and religion—how they comfort the soul and warm the heart! The record God has preserved about the saints—what great men of God in high moments of their lives did and said—these are the sweet heritage of the church. It will be a sad day when we forget them or let them go into the dustbin of forgotten things. But it will be a great day for us when these theological beliefs and heavenly thoughts wake up and become a part of us, so that we begin to make practical use of our treasures.

I have thought of the difference between coal lying in the depths of the earth and coal as it is in the combustion chamber, say, of a locomotive. I think I got this line somewhere in the poetry of another day, "The fury that is coal awake." That doesn't sound poetic, but somewhere it was geared into a poetic line, and I remember it. And I have thought about coal lying asleep there in the heart of the earth. Generations come, generations go, and the coal lies hidden there. Trees grow up and crash down, the grass grows, animals stamp over the hills, men till the soil, and nobody dreams that amazing, astonishing power is lying there just a few feet beneath the surface.

Then one day after uncounted centuries, some men go down in there and take that coal out and carry it across country. Finally it reaches the tender of a great old-fashioned locomotive. It gets into the combustion chamber and creates steam, the steam gets into the cylinders, the cylinders begin to move, and pretty soon that coal which had lain dormant for centuries is pulling a train of a hundred cars, loaded down with merchandise, from one great city to another.

There you see the power and fury of coal wakened from its long sleep. But it must be awakened by fire. It must be awakened in the combustion chamber. It must be awakened by first being blasted out, then pulled loose from its ancient bed and thrown into the fire pit of the locomotive. Then, and only then, it becomes power to pull that great train.

It is so with our theology. It is so with the ideas we hold from the Book of God. It is so with the words that we mull over as sweet morsels in our mouths. It is so with the theological truths and the beautiful spiritual thoughts that are ours in the church of Christ. As long as they lie quiescent and are only ideas, they are of no value in practical life. But when they are thrown into the furnace of faith and obedience they catch fire, and pretty soon the man who was dormant and doing nothing becomes an engine to pull and to do and to stir his generation.

Now, the book of Joshua is a book of "coal awake"; it is a book of doctrine on fire; it is a book of activity born out of doctrine.

Note it says that it came to pass "after the death of Moses." That word "after" and the phrase "the death of Moses" seem to belong together. Joshua had clung to Moses as a young man to an older man, and I have thought that Joshua had leaned on Moses so completely that he felt—instinctively felt—that there could be no "after" when Moses died.

But there was an "after." Moses died, and there was still an "after." An honored leader had to be displaced, and there were a number of reasons for that. One was he was getting pretty old. Another was that God wanted to show Israel that it was not the leader but God Himself who was in charge. God intends an ever-progressing movement forward to an end that is not yet in sight. He sees the end from the beginning, and He sees the end as quickly as He sees the beginning. You and I see only the beginning, and for that reason we need to have faith in the God who sees the end.

God is always moving forward toward a predetermined end. Jesus said, "My Father worketh hitherto, and I work" (John 5:17). We read also in the New Testament of the working of the Holy Ghost. So we know that all three Persons in the blessed Trinity—Father, Son, and Holy Ghost—are working; they are active. God is not a great silent sea, buried in mist. He is an active worker in His universe—at rest but always active; active but always at rest. Doing, to Him, burns up no energy and creates no effort, for God is always God. And He is always doing.

But in this mighty creative activity through the years God must displace leaders with other leaders. Sometimes a Moses must give way to a Joshua. Joshua takes over when Moses lays down his tools.

I have already given two reasons for the change. There is a third. Sometimes God has to displace certain of His leaders when they lose their fluidity; that is, when they cease to be fluid in the hand of God, when they cease to be malleable, when they get a fixed outlook so that what can be is equated with what has been.

Whenever a man's mind becomes static and fixed on what has been, then he can no longer work with God. God says, "Consider not the things of old; lo, I will do a new thing" (see Isa. 43:18–19). And God is always wanting to do new things for His church—new things for His people always. When we become fixed and static and cease to be fluid so that future expectation is equated with past accomplishment, then we have died.

Can't you see, my brethren, that if God is God, what has been is not the same as what will be? God will do anything He has to do or must do to fulfill His purpose. And we must keep our minds open. Churches, gospel organizations, missionary societies—these often stand still for years because they cannot think progressively; they cannot think along with God about tomorrow; they can only think pensively about yesterday.

When a man thinks of yesterday to the neglect of tomorrow he is an old man, regardless of how few birthdays he has celebrated. And as long as a man thinks progressively about the work of God for today and tomorrow he is a young man, however hoary his locks may be or however many birthdays he may have piled up on the calendar.

To stop expecting something better is always tragic in the life of any church or individual. For the way of God with His people is always to outlive one era and enter into another and greater era, moving forward and entering into another and greater era; moving forward always, never standing still. I have never believed much in religious plateaus. I know plateaus exist. I know that in psychology and in private and personal life and also in the Bible there are little plateaus—times when we climb a mountain and arrive happy but worn out. Then God will let us have a little plateau, a little level place where we can rest before we start the next climb.

But those plateaus—we're not to pitch a tent there, let alone build a house. They're just little resting places on the way up. Yet so many of our churches are built on the plateau of past accomplishments. God never intends it to be so. He intends one glorious, victorious era to give way to the next one as fast as we're able to take it—on and on until the Lord comes or until He calls us to be with Himself.

Brethren, I do not believe that we ever ought to superannuate our spirits. It's entirely possible for a man to get sick and old and have to be superannuated, to retire somewhere to sit and meditate the last few years of his life because of broken health. But I do not believe a man ever ought to superannuate his spirit. I do not believe we ever ought to allow our minds or our spirits to get settled—to put on the square hat and get the diploma and say, "Now I have arrived."

No man has arrived until his feet are walking on the golden streets. No man has arrived until the Lord has said, "I'm finished with you on earth, come up higher." Regardless of age, regardless of the passing of the years, regardless of how much we may know—always there is spiritual progress, always there is the going forward, always there is a place farther on.

The church of Christ has never been told that she's retired and that she's to sit down and call it a day. There's always progressive action—always something to do. The doctrines of God are to get on their working clothes, get their hammer and their sword, and go out and get busy. That's the purpose of God for His church.

Now, sometimes we miss God's signal to go ahead and we settle back into a state of quiescence and spiritual inaction. The evidence of this state is that we are then pleased if we can hold our present gains, happy when we can "hold our own."

God's purpose is never for us to hold our own, but always to make some kind of progress. When we fall into the habit of much talk about past victories, when pain goes out of our activities, when we have learned how to do religious work without much cost to ourselves, then we have reached a plateau and it is time for us to stir ourselves and ask God to quicken us again.

> *The doctrines of God are to get on their working clothes, get their hammer and their sword, and go out and get busy. That's the purpose of God for His church.*

I believe that we ought to work with God who "worketh hitherto" and is still working. And if we find that we have temporarily gone out of gear with God, that we're trying to make up for lack of action by much talk—like a man who jacks up his rear wheels, races his motor, burns up the gasoline, and makes a lot of smoke and noise but gets nowhere—I say, if we're in that spiritual state, then by all means we ought to ask God to forgive us and bring us to repentance.

In the Christian life one spiritual advance should follow

another, one stirring up of the nest should follow another, one repentance unto new victory should come after another, one era of fresh, rich, fruitful growth should follow another—on and on during our entire life here on earth, until our Lord Jesus Christ shall come in His glory.

Then we shall meet Him, not as Christians who have already attained, but as Christians who have been growing hitherto and are still growing.

EATOR OF HEAVEN AND EARTH; AND IN JESUS CHRI

S   ONLY   SON,   OUR   LOF

O   WAS   CONCEIVED   BY   THE   HOLY   SPIR

RN   FROM   THE   VIRGIN   MA

FFERED   UNDER   PONTIUS   PILA

S   CRUCIFIED,   DEAD   AND   BURI

SCENDED   INTO   HELL,   ON   THE   THIRD   D

SE   AGAIN   FROM   THE   DE

CENDED   TO   HEAV

S   AT   THE   RIGHT   HA

GOD   THE   FATHER   ALMIGH

ENCE   HE   WILL   COME   TO   JUD

E   LIVING   AND   THE   DE

BELIEVE   IN   THE   HOLY   SPIR

E   HOLY   CATHOLIC   CHUR

E   COMMUNION   OF   SAIN

E   REMISSION   OF   SI

E   RESURRECTION   OF   THE   FLE

REATOR OF HEAVEN AND EARTH; AND IN JESUS CHR

IS ONLY SON, OUR LO

HO WAS CONCEIVED BY THE HOLY SPI

ORN FROM THE VIRGIN MA

UFFERED UNDER PONTIUS PILA

AS CRUCIFIED, DEAD AND BURI

ESCENDED INTO HELL, ON THE THIRD

OSE AGAIN FROM THE DE

SCENDED TO HEAV

TS AT THE RIGHT H

F GOD THE FATHER ALMIGH

ENCE HE WILL COME TO JU

E LIVING AND THE DE

BELIEVE IN THE HOLY SPI

E HOLY CATHOLIC CHUR

E COMMUNION OF SAIN

E REMISSION OF SI

E RESURRECTION OF THE FLE

SOURCES

Foreword: "Tozer's Creed" cites John Oxenham, "Credo,"
in *Bees in Amber: A Little Book of Thoughtful Verse* (London:
Methuen & Co., 1913); Samuel Miller, *The Utility and Importance
of Creeds and Confessions: Addressed Particularly to Candidates for
the Ministry* (Philadelphia: Presbyterian Board of Publication,
1839), 40–41.

Prologue: "Why the Creeds Are Still Important Today"
published as "How Important Is Creed?," in *Alliance Witness*,
August 8, 1950, 2; later published in *That Incredible Christian:
How Heaven's Children Live on Earth* (Chicago: Moody Publishers,
1964), 13–16.

Chapter 1: "God the Father" transcribed from "Attributes
of God—Introduction," a sermon preached at Avenue Road
Alliance Church on January 1, 1961, later published as "God's
Character" in *The Attributes of God, Volume 2* (Chicago: Moody
Publishers, 2003), 1–14.

Chapter 2: "Jesus Christ" part one transcribed from "The
Word Made Flesh—the Mystery of It," a sermon preached at
Southside Alliance Church in Chicago on December 20, 1953;

later published as "The Mystery of the Incarnation" in *Christ the Eternal Son* (Chicago: Moody Publishers, 1982), 7–16. Part two published as "God Walking among Men," in *That Incredible Christian: How Heaven's Children Live on Earth* (Chicago: Moody Publishers, 1964), 37–40.

Chapter 3: "Holy Spirit" published as "The Forgotten One," in *God's Pursuit of Man* (Chicago: Moody Publishers, 1950, 1978), 67–79.

Chapter 4: "Crucified" part one published as "Who Put Jesus on the Cross?," in *Who Put Jesus on the Cross?* (Chicago: Moody Publishers, 1976), 1–11. Part two, "A Note about Christ Descending into Hell," is transcribed from "False Teachings on Obscure Bible Passages," a sermon preached at Southside Alliance Church, June 13, 1954.

Chapter 5: "Resurrected and Ascended" part one published as "What Easter Is About," in *Alliance Witness*, April 17, 1957; later published in *The Radical Cross* (Chicago: Moody Publishers, 2005, 2009), 159–63. Part two published as "The Easter Emphasis," in *Alliance Witness*, March 3, 1959, 2; later published in *The Radical Cross*, 23–26.

Chapter 6: "Returning" transcribed from "Christ's Second Coming," a sermon preached at Southside Alliance Church in Chicago on September 29, 1953. Transcribed and published as "Where Will the Experts Be When Jesus Comes?" in *I Call It Heresy* (Chicago: Moody Publishers, 1991), 156–73.

Chapter 7: "The Communion of the Church" published as "The Communion of the Saints," in *Alliance Witness*, September 12, 1956; later published in *Man, the Dwelling Place of God* (Chicago: Moody Publishers, 1966, 1997), 78–86; also published in *Church: Living Faithfully as the People of God—Collected Insights of A. W. Tozer* (2019), 81–88.

Chapter 8: "Forgiveness" part one published as "Christian, Do You Downgrade Yourself Too Much?," in *The Tozer Pulpit: Book 6* (Chicago: Moody Publishers, 1975),136–48. Part two published as "The Futility of Regret," in *Alliance Witness*, June 13, 1962, 2; later published in *That Incredible Christian: How Heaven's Children Live on Earth* (Chicago: Moody Publishers, 1964), 117–20. Part three published as "Is It True That Man Lost His Franchise to the Earth?," in *The Tozer Pulpit: Book 6*, 105–18.

Chapter 9: "Eternity" part one published as "Faith or Imagination," in *Alliance Witness*, April 6, 1955, 2; later published in *The Price of Neglect* (Chicago: Moody Publishers, 1991), 68–71. Part two published as "Our Hope of Future Blessedness," in *Alliance Witness*, August 13, 1958, 2; later published in *Born After Midnight* (Chicago: Moody Publishers, 1959, 1987), 161–64.

Chapter 10: "Let's Be Humble about Our Orthodoxy" published in *Alliance Witness*, August 1, 1956, 2; later published in *Born After Midnight* (Chicago: Moody Publishers, 1959, 1987), 91–95.

Chapter 11: "Connecting Our Creeds to Our Deeds" published as "Creeds and Deeds," in *Alliance Weekly*, November 7, 1936, 713–14; a shorter version was reprinted in *Alliance Weekly*, October 23, 1943, 679.

Chapter 12: "Doctrine at Work and Going Places" published in *Moody Monthly*, May 1957, 19–20.

*An illustrated edition of Tozer's classic,
designed for discovery, reflection, and sharing*

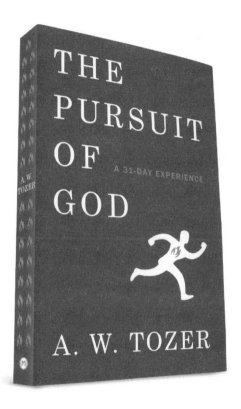

**MOODY
Publishers®**

From the Word to Life®

This illustrated exploration of Tozer's classic
The Pursuit of God is designed for accessible,
slow reading that fosters discovery, reflection,
and sharing. Visually rich and theologically
profound, this edition pairs Tozer's wise words
with graphically paced images that let the reader
encounter divine truths anew and share them
with others.

978-0-8024-2195-1 | also available as an eBook

More timeless, spiritual writings from A. W. Tozer

Christians often know the *theory* of the Spirit-filled life but not the joy-filled *experience*. This timely voice provides a timeless glimpse into spiritual maturity and growth. Tozer wants to ignite a divine fire in our souls. Readers are given sequential steps to living *The Deeper Life*.

978-0-8024-2933-9

Available as eBook and audiobook

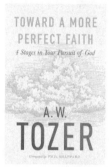

Tozer called these sermons the most important he ever preached. Looking closely at Philippians 3, he describes the Christian as a modern-day Lazarus who hears the call to arise—but can't escape the grave clothes. These sermons usher you into a deeper life of love and maturity in Jesus Christ.

978-0-8024-3070-0

Available as eBook and audiobook

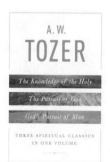

Considered to be Tozer's greatest works, *Knowledge of the Holy*, *The Pursuit of God*, and *God's Pursuit of Man* are now available in a single volume. Discover a God of breathtaking majesty and world-changing love, and find yourself worshiping through every page.

978-0-8024-1861-6

MOODY
Publishers®

From the Word to Life®